THE BATTLE
FOR THE SOUL
OF CANADA

THE BATTLE
FOR THE SOUL
OF CANADA
FIRING THE FORGE

GRANT S ABRAHAM

THE BATTLE FOR THE SOUL OF CANADA

FIRST PRINT EDITION | THE BATTLE FOR THE SOUL OF CANADA | © 2023
1   23

LIBRARY AND ARCHIVES CANADA

ISBN 978-1-7380090-08

Published in Alberta, Canada, by *FiveArrowsMedia.com*.
Design by *JustCreating.ca*.

This book is written in sincere gratitude to all the truckers, farmers, soldiers, freedom fighters, and patriots that stood up for Canada and liberty in this nation.

It is for all the people who came out and gave voice to support the Freedom Convoy from cold overpasses across our country in solidarity with the spirit of freedom. You reminded us of the Canada we grew up in and the values that make it so great.

To all the new Canadians of every creed and colour who came out to the peaceful protest in Ottawa and across Canada to assert your presence in alignment with freedom in this great nation—despite the bullying tactics of this current minority government desperately struggling for legitimacy.

Your sounds harmonize with the true spirit of freedom embedded in this nation's foundation stones and laws, which were carefully set in place to ensure the lasting legacy of freedom here.

What you did then matters—and your voices matter now more than ever.

Canada shall not be forfeited.

Grant Abraham, 28 May 2023.

Ottawa

In the Assembly of Remembrance within the Peace Tower in Ottawa, our forefathers inscribed the following for us:

> ***Justitia Libertas Perpetuo [Justice Freedom Forever]***[1]

> ***"Freedom is the sure possession of these alone who have courage to defend it."*** ***[Pericles]***[2]

We must not choose a false peace purchased by compliance over the freedom that is our birthright as Canadians.

TABLE OF CONTENTS

ACKNOWLEDGMENTS

It is with certainty that I first express my sincere gratitude to my family, Caroline, and our boys, for championing and persevering with me in this effort. It would not have happened without your sturdy support, patience, and encouragement every step of the way.

For all my friends who jumped in without hesitation simply because you believe this discussion needs to happen on behalf of the many Canadians feeling so disenfranchised right now. Thank you personally for this, and I also acknowledge your sincere commitment to our wonderful country and its freedom.

A special thanks to Violet Stockton for holding the torch with your encouragement and ongoing review of multiple drafts through the working journey. You have been a constant and dedicated support, and I humbly thank you.

To Kim Driedger and the whole team at FiveArrowsMedia, my profound thanks for all your work on this; you simply made it better.

1
CHAPTER ONE

| Building an Off-ramp From This Mess

Little by little, Canada is being turned into a perverted version of itself. This diabolical transformation is being accomplished through a strategy to deconstruct the existing value framework, rebuilding it again as a distorted edifice for darkness, poverty, captivity, and tyrannical control rather than light, truth, justice, security, opportunity, prosperity, and freedom.

The Canada we were born in, or embraced for a new life, is being radically undermined and destroyed. Whether you are an old-stock Canadian or a new(er) Canadian, we must be aware of what is at stake and take action now so that this nation does not surrender to this agenda. We are dealing with a threat to our way of life, our sovereignty as an independent nation and our very existence as a people.

The purpose of this book is not so much to debate the above statements but to remind all the disgruntled free-thinking Canadians that while we may be currently fragmented, we are not powerless. If we can find each other and the common ground we cherish, together, we can deploy a united and strategic response to stop this attack on our freedom in its tracks. Only then can we restore Canada to the bedrock values it was built upon and reform this nation so this agenda to deconstruct Canada does not happen again.

This book is for all Canadians who instinctively realize something is seriously wrong and are unsettled by the opportunistic departures from the rule of law that we have recently observed. In sharing my thoughts, I hope to validate your concerns and mobilize you to action. The intolerance of tolerance seems to leave a very small space for anyone to sit on the fence anymore. If this is you, a suggestion would be to first start with Chapters Three and Four.

This book is also for people of all faiths in Canada that understand that there are forces for good and evil in this world and a spiritual reality that impacts the affairs of nations. As you may know, for evil to prevail, the men and women who can identify it must choose to do nothing.[1] If this is you, you may wish to start by reading Chapter Four. We all share the value of family, believing that it is the parents who should make decisions about how their children are raised. We all believe, cherish, and support the right to worship freely, and we share the view that these rights are given to us by the Creator and not by the government.

These are fundamental values to all of us, yet they are being attacked, distorted, and eroded. We need to stand together now—united, to defend these values.

To all those Canadians who are already standing up against this menace to our society, we know you have already paid the price for your patriotism. You are the truckers, the farmers, the soldiers, the medical practitioners, all of the freedom fighters, and those law-abiding pastors that stood up and continue to stand for freedom and truth and were imprisoned for it—patriots all. You reminded us of the best of this country, and I thank you for standing on guard for us.

This book is written for all who call themselves Christian, from every tribe and tongue across this nation—you have a powerful mandate to reflect the peace, light, and love you carry. Canada needs you to boldly shine the light within. It is time for you to mobilize and collapse this separation of the secular and sacred that has kept you hidden in buildings away from the public square. This nation was founded on principles that flow from the supremacy of God. Where are you?

Most importantly, this book is about identifying a shared space where people of all faiths (or no faith) and all patriots can align, converting their individual voices into a united sound of freedom, securing the Canada we will be proud to give our grandchildren.

In order to build toward this vision, we first need an effective off-ramp from the current mess we are in by understanding that there are challenging and awkward issues that have contributed to our current situation because we have simply ignored and avoided having the hard conversations as a nation. We cannot galvanize as a force to define the Canada we want until we can locate each other in the fog created by the current fragmentation of our country. In sharing these thoughts, I hope to help us find each other and understand how we got here in the first place.

These awkward issues are discussed within the respective chapters pointing to and including why the Conservative Party of Canada (CPC) is no longer fit for purpose to meet the challenges Canada is facing today, given the level of

This is a battle for our nation's identity, legacy, and soul.

reform required to correct our course as a nation.

It is my hope that unearthing these matters for discussion now, will help us see how we, as everyday Canadians, have inadvertently contributed to this current attack on freedom in Canada. If we can look honestly upon these root issues in our nation and then come together with a response, we will get the Canada back that is slowly fading and ensure that our freedom is re-established to endure.

We must clearly recognize the gravity of where we are as a nation right now. This is a battle for our nation's identity, legacy, and soul. Whether we can properly discern the threats, how we answer and respond to the questions raised, and if we can unite around shared values will determine whether we stay fragmented, or offer a new and clear sound to Canada that will bring restoration to our land.

It is time to contend for Canada.

CHAPTER TWO

Canada Badly Needs a Conservative Renaissance at the National Level

During the Canada Strong and Free Conference on March 22, 2023, Stephen Harper noted that "Our country is badly in need of a conservative renaissance at the national level" and nostalgically referenced the Conservative Party as a "synthesis" of "the Toryism of Eastern Canada, the populism of the west, and the autonomist tradition of Quebec and French Canadians."[1]

Harper refers to this synthesis as the populist conservatism that formed the Conservative Party that he conceived. If you take the time to listen carefully to Harper's comments from that speech, he both celebrates the 1993 election victory of the Reform Party as a kind of insurgent renaissance that obliterated the footprint of the Progressive Conservative Party and develops the concept of populism, framing it inside the events of the last three years for the Canada of 2023.[2] He goes on to remind his listeners of the original usage and meaning of the word populism as being derived from its late nineteenth-century usage in the Western United States, where the small-business, agrarian 'little guys' stood up to the monopolists and elites of that day, just like we are doing today.

Like a card master strategically positioning playing cards,

there are four very clever sleights of hand in Harper's comments that are all designed to subtly ratchet the 'big blue tent' further, over all the necessary people that it will take to create a pathway to victory for the Conservative Party in the next federal election. Pierre Poilievre needs the tent to be further elasticated as the gaps within conservatism and populism become larger and less easy to reconcile, which is why these comments from Harper are so strategic.

The first manoeuvre was to converge all of the definitions of populism and reinforce their value to the listener as good things. The Reform Party was good. Harper's synthesis that created populist conservatism was good because it won an election. The historical origin of the word was also good. The clear inference is that populism is good, so don't ever discard the populists; Preston Manning was a populist who commenced a renaissance that was being celebrated at the Strong and Free Conference. How could anyone argue with this logic?

The unifying logic is that because populism is such a good thing, anything defined now as being populist can also find a home inside the party originally conceived to capture, contain, and direct the energy of populist conservatism—a great foundation for where Harper was going.

The second trick was to specifically validate the 1993 Reform Party of Canada legacy and reinforce its value in the synthesis. This validation of this group's contribution, of course, includes the significant block of the social conservatives that made up the Reform Party of Canada. It is important to note that the term 'social conservatives' was never actually used in Harper's comments (that I heard) because using the definition of 'populist' has the desired effect of bundling them up and airbrushing them into the encapsulated history of the Reform Party. The quiet point being made is that they are no longer relevant to the thrust of the Conservative Party of Canada today.

The CPC does not want the social conservative values to mess up the simplicity and clarity of the Poilievre message, which is fairly simple: more money in your pocket will give you more freedom. Harper's careful navigation around the term 'social conservative' avoids the prickly pointedness of providing another reminder to the social conservative cadre with the CPC of what the party has *not* done in exchange for their faithful support. Poilievre definitely does not want this kind of reflection point, which will be even more significant for him given the recent Angus Reid poll from March 2023 that provides a low likeability rating for the new conservative leader.[3] While no one seems to want a discussion about social conservative issues, the party definitely does want their vote and is very careful to curate and preserve this fraying connection.

The third trick was to compare the nineteenth-century monopolistic elites (bankers, train company owners, and grain barons) with the elites of today. Anyone reading this will know that these two usages of the term 'elite' are not similar and mean very different things to many people today.

The historical elites sought to increase shareholder value. Our version and current usage of the term elites are those who attend the World Economic Forum (WEF) in Davos and unapologetically seek the demise of nation-states and citizenry in a swap for global governance and compliant consumers (vassals) controlled by a dystopic technocratic tyranny. Suggesting these as only slightly different things is too much of an understatement. It is my sincere hope that Mr. Harper's comparison was based on naïveté.

The fourth stratagem was to develop the now polished-up understanding of the concept of populism to specifically expand the tent pegs a little bit further and implicitly invite those new or remaining populists back into the conservative family.

There have been a lot of different populists mentioned already, but the next sleight of hand will be to direct the group that I will refer to as the remaining populists. This group includes all the freedom fighters, the people that have previously voted for the People's Party of Canada, and the convoy-type people celebrated around the world who are somehow now despised in Canada, at least by the Trudeau government and the narrative-defining media.

The remaining populists have actually been given the clever name of "Convoy Conservatives" by Tasha Kheiriddin in her book, *The Right Path: How Conservatives Can Unite, Inspire and Take Canada Forward*, which is an intriguing exposé into the mind of a Charest-esque conservative from central Canada.[4] I must caveat my comment here by saying that Kheiriddin does not specifically define Convoy Conservatives as I have briefly outlined in the preceding paragraph. The best way I can describe her perspective is to say that she frames them as those Canadians that are somehow of the conservative species of voter but, at the moment, located just beyond the reach of the big blue tent. I take more time in Chapter Eight to explore how this group may well catalyze the galvanizing of the right for the renaissance of Canadian conservatism, a different one than

10

Stephen Harper is anticipating.

I immediately liked this simple identifier of 'Convoy Conservative' for this group because it exemplifies how some believe that the remaining populists—the Convoy Conservatives—are orphans that can't find their way home, just needing the right messaging to bring them back under the big blue tent. Harper must have true Jedi powers because when he called out to the populists at the Canada Strong and Free Conference, I think I honestly felt a tug myself. Tasha Kheiriddin seems to think Pierre Poilievre might be able to dog-whistle these orphans back in—just long enough for Mr. Poilievre to get elected.

These Convoy Conservative folk are not lost orphans; they are awakened patriots who have observed the failures of the CPC and have simply given up on it. They believe that true conservatives have already departed from the party or will depart when they take time to think about this current iteration of the party. They perceive the continual leftward shift and failure to champion the family and religious freedom to reveal a shallow, if not hollow, value-based framework that renders the party unfit to protect the core values of the nation or contend against the corrosive forces degrading Canada.

Suppose these populists were asked to do a risk analysis on conservatism in Canada. I believe that as their views were explored, they would say that both Harper and Kheiriddin should be more concerned about the deep dissatisfaction felt by the current members of the CPC that feel confused, frustrated, betrayed, even abused, and are still in enough denial that they have not gathered the resolve to actually leave the party yet. This latent and pent-up anxiety is secured by fear and shored up by the logic that anything is better than another Trudeau Liberal term of government. The question must be asked: Is this logic enough to install another party also drifting left at a slightly slower pace?

This structural fragmentation in the hull of this ship called the CPC is a real thing—even if unobserved by party mandarins. A large swathe of recently acquired CPC memberships properly signals that something is wrong in Canada, and the Liberals need to be removed—it does not mean they necessarily like the CPC and its current leader or believe the party can fix the root issues after vanquishing Trudeau.

People will go to any dentist if their toothache is bad enough. In this sense, Kheiriddin is correct to question the depth of the new CPC members' loyalty and to worry about their political pedigree as conservatives in her definition of a conservative.

Now is the time for a renaissance of the right, but it will not look like a blue tent being stretched to the seam-splitting limits so the political class embedded in the Conservative Party can be in power for a Harper 2.0 government. It is going to look very different.

There is a movement of citizen patriots that have now awakened, and they know there are profound threats to the very existence of Canada. They also know that trust for the career-curating political class is non-existent, making it no longer possible to justify laying outside with their toes j-u-s-t inside the flap of the blue tent so that the Liberals don't win again.

These patriots have observed that the problems currently facing Canada are about institutional system failures, a political class that has lost its heart to serve and empower the people, a sense of a loss of moorings with the values that built this nation, and a Conservative Party of Canada that is as guilty for what it has not done as the Liberals are for what they have done. This renaissance is here now—it is

There is a movement of citizen patriots that have now awakened, and they know there are profound threats to the very existence of Canada.

happening at the grassroots, and it is coming out of nowhere that is visible to conventional political commentators.

Kheiriddin was president of the Progressive Conservative Youth Federation in the 90s, worked for the CBC, and was the co-chair for Jean Charest's recent leadership campaign in the CPC. She uses the term dog-whistle a lot in her book when she describes the populists and Convoy Conservatives, which is what I unintentionally also just did in the last sentence by ultrasonically telling all the Convoy Conservatives *what* she is.

Kheiriddin has written an entire chapter in her book on populism in Canada.[5] In the world she sees, Poilievre is the populist, and the Convoy Conservatives are a kind of conspiratorial fringe that he may use to get elected as leader, possibly betraying them after the election. She believes all of the voters with common sense (her little dog-whistle to the rest of her Canada) need to be sensibly attracted to the CPC to ensure a path to victory. This won't happen with any associations to the convoy within the CPC. Kheiriddin seems very concerned about all the new conservative members who may not be true conservatives, including another insightful chapter on her conception of conservatism.[6] She seems to feel the word *freedom* is seriously overused and is now contaminated by the Convoy Conservatives, who only embrace a facet of freedom without any notion of the responsibility that is supposed to go with it.

Let me ask you this: What came first? The contamination and neglect of the concept of freedom by the political class and their codependents or the Convoy Conservatives reacting to the loss?

Insinuating that the Convoy Conservatives have a shallow understanding of freedom reveals exactly why the big blue tent will never stretch far enough to bring them in for very long, if at all. The failure to observe this important distinction exemplifies why many people now believe the Conservative Party of Canada is conservative in name only. This is the same kind of logic that must have allowed French citizens to think they could live in a Vichy France as vassals of a foreign power.

Freedom became the heart cry of the convoy because its usage in our *Canadian Charter of Rights and Freedoms* was invalidated by the Liberal Government, undefended by the Conservative Party of Canada and generally diminished and overlooked by our courts.

The dignity of these hardworking Canadians and the singular fervency of the renaissance birthing message of freedom wasn't just misunderstood and resented—it was feared. It is still feared. Feared because they are activated, awake, untamed, impervious to the media narratives, resentful of the rentier class that feeds off of our government's largesse, and are no longer loyal to any particular party, even when threatened with splitting the vote. How else can you explain why the Freedom Convoy is celebrated in Holland, France, and the US yet, allegedly despised so much in Canada?

Many of the Convoy Conservatives I know would proudly wear that badge, caring little about whether they are wooed by Harper or looked upon with suspicion by Kheiriddin as a proxy for the Laurentian elites.

This book is a commentary on the seaworthiness of the Conservative Party of Canada to meet the challenges that appear to have not been anticipated by the party. It asks whether old-stock and new Canadians who value religious freedom, who believe the family to be society's core building block, and who require parental authority to be protected will come to an awareness that the values that built this nation are now being undefended by the Conservative Party of Canada. The social conservatives and the Christian right certainly make up these ranks. While this group may have been able to tolerate the suspension of their values to attain power in the past, they are now being asked to accept the subjugation and persecution of their faiths coupled with being forced to turn a blind eye to the sexualization of children—all while the CPC is silent. How long can this tension last?

The challenge for all Canadians is that we have never been asked about the value deconstruction of our nation;

if we had, we most certainly would have opposed it. So, the stealthy changes have advanced without our consent. These changes are felt by us without us being able to easily locate the source of, or rationale for, the change. For many, the dots still need to be connected. These dots will only get connected, revealing the real story, when the random events of change are plotted within the narrative of the intention behind the change—just like a murder mystery where the facts don't form an explanatory picture until you understand why someone would want to kill.

Justin Trudeau's agenda to transform Canada has certainly been a trigger for these changes, and Covid-19 has been an accelerant, as well as other factors that have contributed to this momentum by the simple omission to act. When looking at all these pieces together, it reveals the targeting of areas where the existing societal infrastructure must be demolished in order for the aspirational agenda to be installed. This aspirational agenda is the deconstruction of the Canada that we grew up in and replacing that with the loss of freedom and with tyranny. Tyranny is the disease of freedom.

Tyranny is emerging in Canada, and we must acknowledge what is happening to our nation for a meaningful and effective response to be brought to arrest the development of this disease, repair the damage, and restore health to our democracy and nation.

In order to do this, we need to be honest about what we have *not* done and what the Conservative Party of Canada has not done to allow us to get to this place. We must be brave enough to ask why so many important cues and clues have been neglected. To be sure, we need a renaissance of conservatism in Canada, but the fundamental question is: can this renaissance of conservatism in Canada come from within the framework of the existing CPC?

I will argue that the CPC cannot birth a renaissance of the Canadian right to meet Canada's current challenges; twenty years ago, it properly recognized the deeper problems and threats facing Canada and simply failed to provide any response before a weed became an infestation. I suggest that the ongoing failure to act was rooted in a begrudging disdain for a large component of its own membership that actually held some of the answers to the threat facing the nation. I contend that economic theory is the wrong tool to counteract the real threat facing Canada and that the Conservative Party of Canada is about to amplify these failures and inadequacies by relying on the same policy platform that permitted the current threat to Canada to birth, form, and thrive in the first place.

Finally, I will implicitly argue how the guiding minds within the CPC have been negligent in not allowing space for this conversation to occur within the party, that they have forfeited the party's mandate to lead, surrendered their legitimacy to steward the security and prosperity of the people of Canada, and may have compromised the sovereignty of our nation in their omissions.

There is another solution.

The untamed energy of the new populists, the Convoy Conservatives, need to be joined together with the disenfranchised grassroots and social conservative Christian right to create a fusion that will be the true antidote to tyranny. The renaissance of the Canadian right will be birthed by those who know that true freedom will be solidified and protected by a sound ideological and value framework that secures generational prosperity instead of promising Canadians more money in their pockets as an election slogan.

3

CHAPTER THREE

The Pathology of Tyranny—How We Got Here and Where This Is Going if We Don't Stop It[1]

In discussions with friends across our nation, there seems to be a collective knowledge that we are in trouble in Canada and that our challenges are existential, even epic. This knowledge comes with the reality that the Canada we used to know has been lost in the ether, without anyone being able to put a finger on exactly what happened or what was stolen. Being aware of this loss finally ushers us toward the vital conversations we must have as citizens and communities.

The truckers, farmers, and veterans unearthed this vague collective impulse for us. They taught us again about unity, regardless of race, and that we are one blood and one nation together. This display of courage, joy, peace, and freedom captured the world's attention, displaying again the attributes we have been so proud to be known for. They evidenced a sort of zeitgeist, coupled with *joie de vivre* that was found in the ragtag community of Canadians from all over the nation, gathering around free food, hot tubs, street hockey games, dancing, bouncy castles, and a knowledge of the true spirit of our *Charter of Rights and Freedoms* during those cold days in Ottawa in early 2022.

The spirit of those days now taunts us with the paradox of what is now our reality with the familiar awareness of what Canada ought to look like. Peaceful demonstrators and pastors sat in prison without bail, reminding us that Canada no longer tolerates disagreement with those in power and a distinct class of Canadians, politely referred to as 'those people', who seem to live in a status of otherness. The invocation of the Emergencies Act and the subsequent vindication of the Liberal Government by Commissioner Paul Rouleau to justify the deployment of militarized police on horseback and the seizing of personal bank accounts only confirms this frustrating paradox.

These inconsistencies and the powerlessness that Canadians feel highlight the desperate condition in the soul of our nation and the awkward reality that millions of Canadians now belong to this loathsome group in our own country. But how did we get here?

From my perspective, the root cause is an intentional attempt to change Canada's long-standing social contract between the individual and the state. The social contract is the invisible arrangement between the individual and the state that explains and rationalizes why a government, or state, exists as an aggregation of the citizen's interests, showing how this relationship is designed to improve and protect the individual, enhancing their freedom. This is not the space for a discussion, but this notion of the social contract emanates from the writing of the minds of Jean-Jacques Rousseau, John Locke, Thomas Hobbes, and other great thinkers.

If you grew up in Canada in 1960 up until even the early 90s, you grew up in a nation where "peace, order, and good government" was the benchmark for the collective public perception of the government—this was the starting point.[2] The government was basically perceived to be impartial and fair; if it wasn't actually morally good, it was at least benign in its intentions.

We grew up in a country where people mostly trusted the government. Poor leadership or bad performance in government were the exceptions to this rule. We relied on the trusted infrastructure of democracy, the balance of powers, and the fairly short leash of the rule of law that constrained the excesses of the state in favour of individual rights. Some may cry naiveté, but this was pretty much the attitude that grew to become the general collective psyche; government basically ran itself, and life didn't change much whether under a Liberal or Conservative government.

Fast forward 25 years to the outbreak of Covid-19 in March of 2020, where some hysteria and fear were amplified by the media, with videos circulating of people falling over dead in China and entire communities being wiped out in Italy. Now you have a global event where humanity was suddenly perceived to be very vulnerable, and governments needed to coordinate their efforts for the good of humanity. Our innocent trust was put in a place where it could be taken advantage of. In leveraging fear, this environment provided the opportunity to formalize this 'reset Canada' and accelerated deployment of a new social contract—a new 'term sheet' for how Canadians relate to and are ruled by their government.

We have to take some responsibility for allowing these things to happen. Let's not forget that we have all been so busy enjoying the benefits of this nation and building our

RRSPs, or whatever, that we neglected to monitor closely what our governors were actually doing. We have omitted to engage, interrogate, or responsibly act for at least two generations since World War 2. I dread what my uncles, who fought and died in that war, would think of our lurch toward tyranny today.

The charming promise of 'sunny ways,' supported by an indecipherable new lexicon of words, introduced Canadians to a hollowed-out language where words could shape-shift their meaning for each new context that the Gumby-like government required. With some added gaslighting, you have a recipe for a kind of subconscious collective denial of change, all while the legacy media perpetuates a spirit of fear across the nation, enhancing dependency on the government.

The evidence for this assertion is abundant. Bedrock values, like freedom of speech, a presumption of innocence, freedom of the press, and due process, are being set aside, or ignored, at an alarming pace. Freedoms enshrined by our forefathers are vaguely disregarded, and sycophantic homage is paid to regimes run by tyrants like the Chinese Communist Party (CCP) or amorphous forms of governance with tenuous accountability to the citizen housed in mechanisms like the United Nations (UN). National sovereignty is passé and it seems democracy may be too cumbersome when self-appointed elites

Fellow Canadians, the legal framework that supports our way of life is being deconstructed and rewritten before our eyes.

think they know better than the people.

The collective, represented by the state, is what matters now in this reset version of Canada—not free citizens holding inalienable rights. Self-sufficiency is out; dependence on the state is in.

The long-promoted and deeply ingrained promise of a better future with honesty, dignity, and hard work is to be replaced by universal income and a new slick definition of prosperity where you share your stuff—for the improvement of all. Your rights and your risk/reward relationship are to be replaced with smothering safety and digital identification to ensure you behave as you are told to.

Fellow Canadians, the legal framework that supports our way of life is being deconstructed and rewritten before our eyes. This brutal truth will never be told to us directly as a statement of policy to vote against until it is too late for us to respond meaningfully. In the meantime, we are disoriented by how language is used, as old and familiar words are given new meanings. Unity now implies alignment with narrow ideological views, inclusion means the exclusion of some, and truth means one thing here and another thing there.

Justice means nothing for the Iranian-Canadians on Ukrainian Airlines flight #752 or the countless Indigenous women lost on the Highway of Tears since 1970. The victim of this gaslighting is truth; the desired outcome is your confusion and insecurity, preventing you from asking, "What the hell is really going on?" People ask this when they have just awakened in the midst of a crisis or walk into a room where there is already a problem brewing. We should not be surprised that this is what is happening—there were multiple warning signs.

Consider the National Security and Intelligence Committee of Parliamentarians *Annual Report 2019* on foreign interference (Pg. 77, Paragraph 189),[3] presented by the Honourable David McGuinty in an oral briefing to the press: "The committee believes there is ample evidence that Canada is the target of significant and sustained foreign interference activities…[that] seek to exploit the openness of our society and penetrate our fundamental institutions to meet their objectives."[4] The report also notes that "Canada is [a clear target, and our] response can be vastly improved."[5] The fact that we are dealing with this same issue nationally at the time of writing this (in the last week of February 2023) following the revelation of the leak by a CSIS agent, who essentially said the same, is nothing other than shocking because in 2020 we had a Liberal MP telling our government this!

In fact, if you go back to 2010, the Director of CSIS, Mr. Richard Fadden, did a CBC interview on foreign involvement in Canada, revealing the penetration of foreign influence into the Canadian government.[6] China was carefully revealed in that interview. No one listened.

It is also fascinating that Justin Trudeau seems more concerned about the leak of the CSIS documents relating to foreign interference in our election process than he does that foreign interference occurred in the first place. While this kind of redirection is not surprising from Justin Trudeau, the more important issue is where were the voices of the Conservative MPs, elevating the issue of foreign interference in the last four years? The answer is that they were essentially nowhere. This report was obviously ignored and buried, but I just can't decide what is worse—to be powerless to do anything about it being buried or that those who knew may be complicit in it. I still choose the former.

Foreign interference is rife. One wonders if it is a coincidence that Klaus Schwab was bragging about the WEF penetrating more than 50% of the current Canadian cabinet. Whenever the name of the WEF comes up, it seems to be readily dismissed as a conspiracy theory. Yet, it is much better organized than many national governments, fusing international governance, the technology sector, media, and health sciences fueled by massive global wealth.

But why would anyone want to unravel, deconstruct, or demolish Canada, you might ask? The intention to have or consume Canada is not difficult to discern in a world with massive populations, limited resources, and exhausted soil like it is in China. In this world, Canada provides bountiful motivation to others in order to influence its policies, control its markets, or simply possess it.

China's strategy is clear through its Belt and Road Initiative (BRI): debt slavery and control in the developing world. Why would the core strategy be different anywhere else? If you have done any work in China, you will understand the political psyche emanating from the concept of what the Middle Kingdom actually means. Insightful research has been produced on the access, influence and subversion of developing countries by the Chinese. You may also take the time to review Clive Hamilton and Markicke Ohlberg's book called: *Hidden Hand: Exposing How the Chinese Communist Party is Reshaping the World.*

The destruction of national sovereignty is at the very

heart of the World Economic Forum, and the fact our current Prime Minister is telling us that "This pandemic has provided an opportunity for a reset" should be a clue for us,[7] especially when set beside the name and further disorientating language of Klaus Schwab's book, *The Great Reset.*[8] Deputy Prime Minister Chrystia Freeland also sits on the Board of Directors of the WEF.

The Greek philosopher Pericles famously said, "I am more afraid of our own mistakes than of our enemies' designs." Churchill warned Britain, still numb by the First World War, of Hitler's true intentions to dominate—and more. Canada has been numbed by 80 years of softness, not having to protect our borders while forgetting the balance, values, and synergy emanating from our foundation stones that formed and built this nation. How can we be responsible for defending our values when we have forgotten their sounds?

Our *Charter of Rights and Freedoms* clearly defines these foundation stones: *Whereas Canada is founded upon principles that recognize the supremacy of God and the rule of law.*[9]

The first is the hot forge from which our inalienable rights as citizens emanate. The second is the anvil that shapes our law, ensuring we love our neighbour as ourselves and not do harm to others. It is a sacred synergy, not much discussed anymore. Perhaps God has gone out of fashion, but whether you believe in God or not, these Judeo-Christian principles have set the civic-moral order for the most successful, free, and democratic nations the world has ever seen, including Canada. They should not be quickly abandoned for the impulses of revisionist historians or a thespian, even if you don't believe in God.

If you want to know what is going on and are interested in the pathology of our nation's decline into tyranny, ask yourself if you believe we got here because of the ideological leadership of just one person in the Prime Minister's office.

When my wry friends in Newfoundland refer to our current Prime Minister, they simply call him 'JT'. I like this off-the-cuff Gaelic irreverence—it distinguishes between the man and the role without besmirching the high office meant to serve our people.

If one continues with this clever parsing, it begs the question of whether there is another distinction to be made between the presence of this stage actor (JT) and the enduring longevity of the possibly treasonous plan to turn Canada into a post-nation state.

We must ask ourselves: If we get rid of this man, do we get rid of the plan?

I think the answer to that question is no, but your answer really depends on whether you believe it is plausible that JT devised these groundbreaking changes to our nation on his own and then cunningly advanced them by wit, intellect, and by force of will.

It is an awkward question for us all because our trusting nature, or perhaps selfishness, wants the answer to be that our current situation was all JT's idea, so this can all go away when he does. The duty to our nation requires us to ask whether JT had help or whether a more sophisticated plan has been strategically in place for some time.

Perhaps an oversimplified metaphor might help. This nation needs to decide if JT just had a bad night out on the town, got drunk and accidentally drove his car into a power station knocking off the electricity for the town and making the local bank vulnerable to a robbery. Or did he just drive into the power station because he was helping his friends in turning off the electricity so they could rob the bank?

It is much more likely that JT is a feckless politician playing a role as the leading straw man who is actively supported by others within the Canadian political class and other domestic and foreign players conspiring to turn Canada into a prototype for how a Western nation can be transitioned away from democracy to become a vassal state of foreign powers. Since writing this last sentence in February 2023, Liberal MP John McKay, in the week of March 6, 2023, has called China an "existential threat," announcing of the Chinese government that "Another government wishes to turn us into a vassal, subservient state, a state where the belt and road literally apply to us. All roads lead to Beijing, and the belt is for our neck. That is the ultimate goal of the government of Beijing; stirring up chaos in our country is the technique."[10]

If you don't like this line of thought, stop reading. I would rather say this and be wrong than ignore what is becoming a clear prima facie case for this agenda to sell Canada out and betray our people.

Consider that in 2015, the *New York Times* quoted JT as saying there's "no core identity" in Canada, and he sees the country as "the first postnational state."[11] The real challenge with this statement for Canadians was that very few people knew what post-nationhood actually meant in North America and how this statement would foreshadow the beginning of the erosion of the country so loved by its citizens.[12]

Post-nationalism means that your governance actually occurs from somewhere other than your national, or provincial, capital and with people that you did not vote for and may not be able to actually identify as the source of decisions made about your city, province or nation. People who desire this are called 'Globalists.'

Consider that in November 2020, just after JT was telling us that "This pandemic has provided an opportunity for a reset,"[13] he was also signing Canada up for the *Agile Nations Charter,* which is a charter co-sponsored by the Organization for Economic Cooperation and Development (OECD) and the World Economic Forum (WEF).

While anything these days that is connected with Klaus Schwab and the globalist agenda of the WEF is deemed to be a conspiracy theory, Canada is a signed-up, active collaborator in this program as well as the Known Traveler Digital Identity (KTDI) with Holland, Air Canada, and the WEF. When will we start seeing past the labelling of these important changes and partnerships being called 'conspiracy theories?

Our participation in the Agile Charter has only recently come to our national attention, with MP Leslyn Lewis astutely picking up on the references to it in the working papers of the government and then digging deeper. Why wasn't Canada told about this in November 2020? What else don't we know?

Consider that Canada has now empowered the World Health Organization (WHO) to both define when a pandemic exists and when to step in, steering our federal response to any other health emergencies.[14] When you take note of the fact that your health information is shared with the WHO, you may wish to start asking why this would be necessary and what the privacy issues are if you don't agree with the future treatments prescribed by the WHO when they declare another pandemic in Canada. The WHO is a direct operational subsidiary of and is embedded within the UN—in case you did not know.

Think about the advance of the UN Agenda 2030 being marketed by the WEF under a general banner of sustainability. The implications of Agenda 2030 for our understanding of ownership, wealth, prosperity, and land rights are staggering.[15] There is a clear correlation between the WEF's marketing statement that "You'll own nothing. And you'll be happy." and the UN Agenda 2030 if you take the time to read it closely.[16]

Please note that the forerunner to Agenda 2030 was Agenda 21,[17] which was birthed at the Rio Summit in 1992 where Canada was represented at this summit by Jean Charest— the same Jean Charest that was positioned to lead the Conservative Party of Canada (CPC) by Red Tories within the CPC in 2022.

If you think the UN Sustainable Development Goals are irrelevant to Canada, or your way of life, consider that for some time now, a team (52 of them) from various levels of civil servants and elected officials in BC have been working on policy positions to have BC restructured to align with Agenda 2030. I will engage this topic more deeply in Chapter Five, but I have had the sad opportunity to review some of this group's working papers provided by someone who was actually a member of this team.

These working papers are titled *Advancing Sustainability in BC* and read like the working papers of a policy committee of the actual government—except they are produced in the shadows, completely away from the scrutiny of parliament, within a not-for-profit organization.[18]

This group is substantively funded by the Liberal Government, with donations in one year adding up to approximately *six million dollars* of taxpayers' money to do this work. This working committee's agenda is to "redesign the systems in which our society operates," including our economic system, education, physical infrastructure, and legal governance.[19]

On the surface, the purpose of this working committee is to advance sustainability, but they have noted that first, they need to redefine our expectations by reviewing concepts like 'prosperity' and 'wealth' because we have 'blind spots' in our worldview that will need to be deconstructed for them to do their work.[20]

Really? This is social reprogramming by a policy-writing think tank that is rewriting our laws and the values of our nation that support our laws. I call this a conspiracy to commit treason—treason and the misappropriation of taxpayers to pay for it when there is no mandate from the people to undertake this work. *This is insidious and provides a heart-stopping glimpse into the line of travel for this nation.*

The UN Declaration on the Rights of Indigenous People (UNDRIP) is also intentionally being folded into this sustainability agenda.[21] I can't help but think that UNDRIP is setting up Canada's First People for betrayal, especially if there are caveats within UNDRIP that would see tribal land transferred to the UN in the event of performance defaults or dispute resolution protocols. This topic is too big to engage fully here but warrants a closer examination so that our Indigenous citizens are not betrayed and our sovereignty is not undermined.

All of the above have the makings of the perfect crime. A well-formed plan constructed over decades and accelerated by fear, in order to attain a massive national treasure with unlimited resources set in a pristine environment and guarded by dozy, soft guards not believing they would ever be robbed. While this is happening, an element of our people is recklessly (and very possibly traitorously) enabling this theft, all while they distract the nation with ridiculous conversations and a general disdain for most of the Canadian people.

The victim is you, your family, your wealth, your security, and your liberty. Collectively, the victim is our sovereignty, our way of life, and our nation.

For anyone that can see what is happening, the motivation to stop this is not the issue. Many are keen to, and I have heard of many plans that consistently fail to identify the root issue, similar to picking the head off of a weed only for it to return a week later. We must recognize how all the matters itemized in this chapter highlight an attack upon specific values cherished within Canada.

Privacy is eroded with the empowerment of the WHO and the sharing of our medical information. Freedom of movement is curtailed by the WEF digital identification pilot programs. Agenda 2030 and the concepts built into and around sustainability are rewriting the understanding of property ownership and how prosperity is understood for building wealth. The UN, the WHO, and the WEF are diluting our comprehension of the national sovereignty of our people and borders. The shrinking popularity of the Liberal Government appears to be facilitating all of this and is shored up by the foreign interference of the People's Republic of China in our democratic process after factually ignoring warnings about foreign interference from their MPs.

Each of these is its own construction site of change, representing a value that has defined Canada and how we live and function as a people. All are very busy unravelling our understanding of each value.

While these changes relate to our nation, changes are happening to our daily life and the things we care about—like our family and our faith or what we can say or even think. These construction sites relate to values like freedom of speech, religion, the press, and our right to raise our children or how we raise our children. When or where we worship and whether faith is now just a privilege that the government can take away. These fundamental rights and freedoms are being clipped, curtailed, diminished, and weakened. We can see it, but we don't explore why it is happening or how the value system is changing. Until we do this, we will not be able to stop what is happening to fix and rebuild the areas where construction to change the nation has already started.

Values really matter and will matter more when we reflect on where the changes are taking us. We need to wake up.

4

CHAPTER FOUR

Values Matter: Money Is Important, but So Is Family, Security and Religious Freedom

Why is faith pushed to the margins of Canadian politics when it is such a core part of so many people's lives and their value frameworks?

This question draws upon Stephen Harper's observations of the dark shift on the left of the political spectrum to a moral nihilism, where there is an actual hatred of the moral framework that built Western civilization.[1] We are now observing what a shift to the darkness of moral nihilism looks like in Canada, and important questions need to be asked about how and why this happened and how we can stop it.

Religious freedom is a pillar of Canadian democracy.

A study published by Statistics Canada in 2019 reports that 68% of Canadians over the age of 15 adhere to a religious faith—furthermore, 54% admitted that "they considered their religious or spiritual beliefs to be somewhat or very important to how they live their lives."[2]

This means that 68% of Canadians derive their value framework from some kind of a transcendental understanding of the spiritual, that this understanding informs their worldview on a moral paradigm where things are perceived in terms of light and darkness, or good and evil.

Sacred to many faiths is the value of the family, the sanctity of life, the stewardship of the environment, and the need for a justice system that protects the innocent and punishes the guilty. There are common perspectives about the family unit with principles that are understood across all faiths: the vulnerable are to be protected, the innocence of children is to be shielded and cherished, and our elders are to be honoured and respected. The family is a bedrock value in Canada and is understood to be the foundation for the building of strong communities and nations.

How is it that so many people who hold similar views can be so marginalized and fragmented while the values they commonly share are picked apart and downgraded?

Parental authority is a key piece in the important role of the family in Canadian society and how our children are raised. Governments have a role to support raising children, but we don't want the government telling us *how* to raise our children. There is a big distinction here where we find that the government is blurring the lines on how far-reaching its authority is with regard to our families. We definitely don't want the sexualization of our children to occur through educational policies or influencer interactions like the drag queen reading programs geared towards children of any age, especially children between 0 and 8 years old. We recognize that the term minor-attracted person (MAP) is a repulsive sanitizing of the word pedophile.

Yet these things are happening in Canada, enabled by government policies that are being advanced at a fanatical pace and without the challenge of these many voices acting in concert together.

Take, for example, Quebec's Bill 15 and how this Bill is taking health policy matters in this direction.[3] We care deeply about who makes the medical decisions for our children's lives, and this policy is a disgusting shift toward the idea that our children ultimately belong to the state rather than their parents. The primary duty of care reverses in this policy, with the state possessing the ultimate authority for children while permitting the parents to act as guardians of the children as they are raised, providing that the parents cooperate and align with state policy. If you stop cooperating, you risk losing your child to the state.

Or take the Conversion Therapy provisions of Bill C-6 (2021), later named Conversion Therapy Bill C-4, where parents can be criminally prosecuted for talking to, counselling with, or praying for their own children regarding matters of gender identity or transitioning discussions.[4] Under this Bill, parents can go to jail for five years if the parents believe biological sex defines gender and they counsel their child in this manner.[5] In comparison, a person that sexually molests a child in Canada will likely only receive *three years* in jail under our Criminal Code and current sentencing rules.

The injustice of these scenarios is gut-wrenching, and realizing what the juxtaposition says about our society is simply sickening. The time for *going along to get along* with this kind of moral logic must end now.

If you think this is a Liberal Government policy and we can just resolve the feeling of disgust by removing them, please know that the MPs from the Conservative Party of Canada *all* voted to enact Conversion Therapy Bill C-4 in 2021.[6] All of them, including Pierre Poilievre, Leslyn Lewis, and the party, did this unanimously under Erin O'Toole's leadership. Please, think about that. There is more in Chapter Five on why the Conservative Party of Canada is no longer a seaworthy ship to guide and protect, let alone champion, religious values or the interests of social conservatives in Canada.

The support of the entire Conservative caucus for this particular Bill is troubling enough, but I recently listened to a presentation by three Conservative MPs—Ed Fast, Tako Van Popta, and Michael Cooper—on May 25, 2023, in a public presentation in Langley, BC who were commenting on the Medical Assistance In Dying (MAID) legislation being designed for Canada. The Honourable Ed Fast made many insightful comments in opposition to this legislation but concluded by saying, "We as Conservatives are the only ones that are allowed free votes to vote in every single matter of conscience."[7] The room erupted in applause at this comment, taking comfort in the value guardrail put in place to allow freedom to vote on important matters of conscience.

This raises another awkward question: How do we reconcile the protection of an MP's conscience or those of their constituents with the unanimous support of Bill C-4? Surely parental authority for the protection of your child's sexual identity and genitalia is a matter of conscience!

I believe what Mr. Fast said is factually accurate and that he also believes it to be true. The only explanation is that some matters appear to be defined as a 'matter of conscience' to enable MPs to vote freely—other matters are not so defined. This begs the question: why was Bill C-4 not classified as a matter of conscience? The deeper and more difficult questions are: why did all of the Conservative caucus fail to identify it as a matter of conscience and then also vote to support it? It is easy to see why those within the CPC membership are so confused about the rationality of the Conservative Party. This is what happens when guard-rail values, like ensuring votes for matters of conscience, morph into marketing gimmicks.

We are enabling career politicians who have taken a lifetime to curate their own importance, leading us to believe that our national problems will be solved, or threats to our children removed, or our parents will be safer in their care facilities if we can just lower taxes, or give Canadians more disposable income.

The flimsy inference is that more money means more freedom. Yes, there is much that can be done economically to unleash the wealth of Canada for Canadians, but it will mean nothing if the nation changes so much that we can't send our children to school because of value dissonance in the curriculum or we can't send our parents to the hospital because they may be counselled toward MAID and just be euthanized.

Values matter.

Hell on earth must be where the state stops you from protecting your child because they think they were born in the wrong biological body and want to mutilate or cut off their genitals.

Another staggering development in this quest to assault and destroy our precious young people is the proposal to extend euthanasia to our children. If you are a parent, you might learn about this "treatment" to your child only in the baffling scenario "where appropriate" for you to know about it and if your child is deemed to have the requisite decision-making capacity on assessment.[8] This is some language of the Special Joint Committee on Medical Assistance in Dying, a parliamentary committee of the Government of Canada (circa February 2023)![9]

My hope is that we can observe and change this before someone gets a call to tell them their son or daughter has died because the government gave their child the right to make medical decisions without parental consent. It is one of the most shocking things that while a parent may not even be notified, our government also takes on the role of counselling the child in those decisions.

Do you think you will be worrying about your RRSP, inflation, or the cost of housing when you get that news? Any parent I know would risk all of their money, their total personal liberty, and their personal life to protect their children. When we know this is true, why would we enable Pierre Poilievre to promise us more money in exchange for power when it is apparent that the challenges we are facing are so much more complex than just being about money?

If we want to stop this assault on our children and the value of the family, we need to look and think more deeply about what is going on. We need to realize that the current government is now a moral actor that is no longer morally neutral as they advance moral principles that radically clash with values held by Canadian people—from many faiths and no faith.

Before leaving office, Prime Minister Stephen Harper recognized the emergence of the moral principles that clash with so many faiths in Canada.

He said,

> "Conservatives need to reassess our understanding of the modern Left. It has moved beyond old socialistic morality or even moral relativism to something much darker. It has become a moral nihilism—the rejection of any tradition or convention of morality, a post-Marxism with deep resentments, even hatreds of the norms of free and democratic western civilization."[10]

This chapter began by acknowledging that 68% of Canadians hold a religious faith and have a transcendental understanding of right and wrong, good and evil. Having a transcendental understanding means there is an awareness of a spiritual realm where an eternal struggle between good and evil exists and impacts our temporal realm.

Can you see that Harper's comment actually described evil, but he did it in philosophical language that was morally neutral and politically correct? Why not just call dark, moral nihilism that hates the norms of freedom—evil? Or the enemy of a free and prosperous democracy? Our grandparents had the moral courage to call Hitler evil. Harper's response was to develop and release tax credits to support families.

It is important to understand that evil doesn't mind being

identified in an innocuous, morally neutral way because there is no pronouncement by another moral value system that judges it to be wrong or requires correction. This is especially true when evil can continue with its agenda shrouded in the camouflage provided by political correctness, ensuring the sacred is not permitted in conversations where the agenda is predetermined to be secular. Wolves that are dressed in sheep's clothing don't mind being harmlessly described as mammals that identify as herbivores—but try calling them a wolf, thereby imputing the intentional bloodlust of a wolf, and they revert to their true disposition.

Most people have not awakened enough to see this yet. Those that are awake have not been permitted to judge a wolf to be a wolf and then take the appropriate steps to ensure its intentions are neutralized. Shrinking from evil by ignoring it, moving out of its way, or just raising a shield to mitigate its impact will no longer work in Canada; history has taught us this. Evil always tries to get good people to tolerate it, who only resist by using a shield until finally backed into a corner and there is nowhere left to move. This highlights the constraints put on our public discussions, and I am guessing this is also why Harper did not just refer to this hateful moral nihilism simply as evil.

Canadians must be permitted to say something is evil or wrong if it offends their sense of right and wrong due to the values they hold. The fact that the root system of those values is derived from a religious perspective is immaterial. Slavery was morally evil because all people were created equal in God's image, among many other reasons. William Wilberforce changed the law on slavery across the British

Empire, and Abraham Lincoln saw it enacted in the United States at a great price because it was right. Do we have the same resolve to properly identify evil and then stop it?

Good people stood for their convictions, and evil was crushed in those confrontations because there was no accommodating space for both perspectives. By starting to have real conversations, we can fortify the true value of religious freedom in Canada and avoid the nasty confrontations that will follow if we do not.

In subsequent chapters, I will ask in more detail whether the Conservative Party of Canada is even capable of having conversations about morality because it seems they have a limiting blindness that only allows the guiding minds within the party to see the security and health of a nation through an economic lens. This aperture is too narrow, and the restricted vision has given us a surging moral agenda advanced by the Liberals and the NDP that the Conservative Party is either ill-equipped to respond to or is simply comfortable with since it does not encroach upon their economic policy agenda in any direct financial way.

Either reason explains why it doesn't matter to the Conservative Party of Canada if there is a law that stops parents from talking to their children about the sex they were born with or their sexuality in general. It may not matter to the policy pundits within the party whose only calculus is re-election—but this sure matters to the members of the Conservative Party who see things from a socially conservative perspective and who likely respect or hold deeply significant religious values. Can you justify advancing economic policy at the expense of family values when the stakes are this high?

Why have we been so naive to think that an attack on parental authority, the innocence and security of our children, the freedom of our religions, or the sanctity of life of our aging parents can be repelled by economic policy alone? If you listen carefully to Pierre Poilievre, you will hear the panacea solution constantly repeated, promising more money in your pocket so you have more freedom to make the choices you want about your life. The problem is revealed when you consider that having more money to defend yourself from criminal charges because you contended for your daughter not to remove her breasts does not make you more free—it means you can afford a lawyer.

More money does not always mean more freedom. No amount of money will return lactating breasts to your daughter or granddaughter to enable her to breastfeed her baby someday if she wishes to. The fact you had the funds to defend yourself against the Crown Prosecution will be of no comfort here. The more important point is that the reason we protect minors with the 'rule of law' is that we know how impulsive and short-sighted we were as children and later grateful for our second chances—young people need to be allowed to change their minds as they grow and not wreck their lives with irreversible decisions.

Pierre Poilievre and all the elected Conservative caucus voted to support this heinous Bill C-4 when they did not have to. Instead of condemning it as misguided, questionable, unsafe, a challenge to parental authority, destructive to family values, or simply a bad idea—they voted for it unanimously.

Economic policy is only a tool. It must never replace or distract from the moral framework that is its master. Pierre

Poilievre's repeated promise to put more money in your pocket is the solitary note of a Pied Piper that will lead the values of this nation over a cliff, leaving us in a morally nihilistic place, as identified by Harper.

Can you see that Harper's limitation in defining the response to this threat by simply defaulting to economic policy to strengthen the family is being formulaically repeated in the shallowness of Poilievre's platform? Harper was able to discern the threat—Poilievre doesn't care about it because it dilutes the purity and simplicity of the Conservative Party's messaging and its calculus for power.

If you believe that parental authority, the innocence of our children, freedom of our religions, or the sanctity of life can be defended by a leader who does not see or understand the moral implications of ignoring them while blindly talking about economics, you will be used for your vote and politely placated when you raise these important issues in policy discussions.

Let me remind all of the Conservatives and the patient members of the Manning Reform party that when the Harper administration fixed the economic issues of that premiership, he never bothered to get to the moral issues that were supposed to temporarily be set aside, in order to forge a pathway to power for the then new Conservative Party. Your vote was used, your patience was relied upon, and your values were brazenly ignored—

Economic policy is only a tool. It must never replace or distract from the moral framework that is its master.

and still are.

If one believes that removing Justin Trudeau and putting more money in your pocket is a good enough solution to move the country forward, the decline of what we truly believe to be important, sacred, and valuable is inevitable. When evil is left unchecked, it grows bolder and takes more ground. Unless it is challenged, it is just a matter of time until your security and freedom live in compounds behind wire.

The antidote to the decay or decline of our nation is people of all faiths who understand these values in Canada, standing up together and confronting it. We need to think about what unites us and build the kind of Canada we want to live in and give to our grandchildren. If we secure the bedrock values and protect our families, the financial blessing of this nation will follow, building the wealth and prosperity that Canada promises and so many hope for and work hard to attain.

This situation has been created because we have allowed ourselves to be fragmented as a people and have bought into the deception that closely held sacred or moral values should not be permitted in the secular political dialogue. We must not permit ourselves to be locked out of the conversation while diabolical moral values are advanced under the veneer of empowerment by a morally compromised government or political parties that can't properly discern what is happening—or don't care. The hypocrisy of this is staggering. Why we have allowed it is shameful.

The division of the secular and the sacred has been used to isolate and marginalize huge components of our society for long enough. The hypocrisy of stopping one section of society from engaging in a moral discussion, because the baseline of their position is predicated upon religious values, is premeditated and self-serving. Sniffy and indignant political correctness wraiths can no longer be permitted to define the scope of dialogue for us when these matters are being challenged.

Together, we will reverse these ridiculous laws (and other legal encroachments on how we want our nation to work) if we unite on the simple premise that freedom is our birthright and, as free men and women, we need to contend for that freedom through the advancement of values that have served the nation so well.

Then, if we can find ourselves spread across the Canadian political spectrum and unite, we finally need to ask ourselves whether the longstanding political parties can deliver the Canada we desire to secure the authority of parents, the lives of the vulnerable, and the respect and care of our elderly as well as ensuring the nation is secure, creating pathways for opportunities, unleashing the wealth of Canada for Canadians. If we can galvanize our shared viewpoint, we can shape Canadian politics and build a nation where we can live in peace and security, with equal opportunities, prosperity and justice.

5

CHAPTER FIVE

The Problems With the Conservative Party of Canada: Why the Conservatives Do Not Have the Answers

If the Liberals can mess up the country this badly with a minority government, why can't an aggregation of the social conservative Christian right and others fix it within a minority government?

The Conservative Party of Canada is a ship built for another era. It was hobbled together with Western Canadian reformers, Alliance Party members, and the fragments of the old Conservative Party, including the fiscally minded Tories, both Red and Blue. Pragmatism prevailed in this union, built upon the argument that the right would not attain the power of the Prime Minister's Office if the divisions persisted, enabling the vote to be split. Fear was used to compel alignment and unification so that the vote would no longer be split and power would be the reward. Power did follow for the Harper administration, but this fear of splitting the vote is still deployed to silence any conversation that challenges the calculus of this pragmatism.

Many important issues to Canadians were shelved because of this rationale, and the fiscal and social conservatives within the current party are still holding their noses when they are together, seduced by power and resentful of the diluting compromises they have to make with each other to get it.

The implicit question posed within this chapter is whether Canadians on the right (and specifically people of religious faith or simply social conservatives) can still justify this pragmatism in order to attain power? This question is even more poignant, especially when the last three elections have been lost without a significant splitting of the social conservative and Christian right vote. It seems the Liberals are getting a lot of very bad things done, even with a minority government.

Perhaps a minority government made up of parties from the right could radically course-correct Canada toward truth, justice, and freedom with a clear intention of restoring and securing the nation.

Canada is in a violent storm, and the seaworthiness of this CPC ship is the biggest challenge facing Canadians on the right of the political spectrum. The free, the strong, and the proud Canada that was supposed to be entrenched and protected by our *Charter of Rights and Freedoms* has been stripped of these certainties and is on the tipping point of becoming a proto-type for globalist feudalism and technological captivity supported by the Internet of Things (IoT).

These issues don't even appear to matter to the Conservative Party of Canada. Digital Identification, 15-minute cities, Known Traveler Digital Identity (KTDI), and facial recognition currently being tested to fly from Vancouver to Winnipeg[1] are all a part of a web being woven for our bondage. The CPC has been the Loyal Opposition for the entire time, but they have not spoken out against *any* of these issues to protect our privacy or query the rampant foreign interference that was astonishingly highlighted to us in 2019 on YouTube, as referenced below.

The real issues are what we are not talking about.

This storm and the ability of the CPC is the only conversation that matters right now to the Canada that does not want to be reset. The wise, free, awake, and canny Canadians know this very well, but the CPC can't, or won't, have this conversation. Why? Because it does not officially recognize that there are threats other than the repetitive narrative about the national debt, inflation, and house prices.

The Conservative Party leadership debate hosted in Edmonton on May 11th, 2022, was a fantastical event, not because of what was said, but rather what was not talked about.[2] Questions about our national sovereignty in light of the authority given to the UN (especially in the context of our health within a transnational UN architecture), why it is we had an election in 2021 and never asked JT what his reset was actually about, or whether it is a good idea for Canada to be a post-nation state—it was all absent from the discussion. How is it possible that those questions were not asked?

How could the simple existence of those statements by a Canadian Prime Minister not prompt an interrogation of what this meant for the people of Canada in a Conservative Party Leaders' debate?

This debate was carefully curated to avoid these important questions being raised. At its very best, this failure to entertain these conversations is a reckless disregard for the sacred duty of the Loyal Opposition. Why haven't we talked about it? Either the party and its governing minds were oblivious to these matters as real issues, or the topics were simply suppressed. I am honestly not sure which one is worse.

Canadians definitely wanted to talk about these issues. I know this because I was talking about these issues in my bid for the leadership of the CPC in 2022. I never left BC and Alberta in that campaign, and as it built up steam, nearly $200,000.00 came into the campaign in the last 48 hours. This money came in from all over Canada to put me over the $300,000.00 entrance fee *because* I was addressing these very issues. The grassroots intuitively knew the truth when they heard it and chose to hope again in a reformed CPC for the challenges facing it and Canada.

To her credit, Leslyn Lewis is now starting to talk about some of these issues as well, but one has the impression that she is constrained from within the party and that her comments are only tolerated in order to placate the social conservatives.

While Pierre Poilievre appears to be silent on these matters, with a clear preference for only talking about quantifiable matters like inflation and the cost of housing, he gives very little oxygen to matters that cannot be established by statistics. Canada's problems right now are not with money per se—they are rooted in the value disconnection between the people and the policies that are making the country unidentifiable.

The existing challenges facing the CPC are many and seem to be embedded in their relationship with their own grassroots, with the elasticized theatrics displayed in the transition from Party Leadership Election to National Election and the continual omitting of particular issues important to social conservatives.

Forgotten values and an identity devalued.

The people of faith within the CPC must be so tired of having their deeply held spiritual values bundled up and labelled as 'just the social conservatives'. There now seems to be a kind of begrudging tolerance within the party that has moved from simply being viewed as tedious to no longer acceptable. Many, if not most, of the issues in this category, emanate from deeply held religious values that define how we want our children to live, our parents to be treated when they are frail, or other moral or religious values embedded in our Charter.

These soul issues have been marginalized and subjugated to the elevated value of fiscal conservatism. Why is this allowed to happen? This hobbled-together partnership has become so one-sided that it is starting to feel abusive in practice while values that people of faith hold dear are ignored or worse.

For a long time, I thought this was just political pragmatism on the part of Stephen Harper as leader of the great merger that birthed the current iteration of the Conservative Party of Canada. Many believed Harper would deal with the obvious, low-hanging economic problems in the nation when he took power, and then he would get to the tough issues that the social conservatives traded their fealty for in

> *What matters now is discerning whether the Conservative Party is actually able to champion these important issues for Canadians in this current environment.*

the new partnership. This never happened. Maybe Harper got tired, or maybe he leveraged the reformers as a pathway to power.

What matters now is discerning whether the Conservative Party is actually able to champion these important issues for Canadians in this current environment. We may also need to ask whether the culture of the CPC has been so indoctrinated by Harper's model and pathway to the Prime Minister's Office that it has created a culture where Harper's model has just become a learned behaviour. Can a Harper 2.0 model work when the root issues are not economic?

A Learned Behaviour

I came across a quote from a very young MP in the Harper caucus who gives an interesting insight into the perspective, or the internal optics of the CPC, on the topic of the social conservatives—specifically the founding reformers' role in the partnership. He said:

> "This is the interesting story of Stephen Harper... Everyone thinks he seduced the centre. It's actually the way he tamed the right...He's now taken the most left-wing position of any conservative party in the world on gay marriage...Harper has ruled out any abortion

legislation. He has basically moved the party onto an agenda that is centrist and acceptable to mainstream people. And he's done it almost without a peep from the right – from the people who founded the Reform Party, who had made the bombastic and even embarrassing remarks that had come to typify the Reform era. All of those people have gone along with this swift, centrist move while making almost no sounds at all."[3]

This statement is tremendously relevant for us now because it reveals an attitude that was allowed to be birthed and later celebrated within the organizational culture of the Conservative Party of Canada. At its core, this acknowledges the actual betrayal of the religious and moral values that are significant to so many good people who had helped birth the CPC and then put it in power.

What is most damning about the above quotation is that it was made by Pierre Poilievre in 2006.

There is much to reflect on here.

As much as Stephen Harper is venerated for his service to Canada, he never did engage those important value issues to the social conservatives. These are the very things they trusted him to champion in exchange for the deal to forge the new party. They gave their vote in exchange for Harper's implied promise to advocate for those issues. That was the *quid pro quo*.

Many Canadians will need to believe that Harper simply ran out of time and was not able to advance the social conservative issues rather than begin the painful process of considering that there never was an intention to do so.

What appears to have happened in this transaction is that the social conservative Christian right got polished up to become centrists who were acceptable to the mainstream. While I am not at all sure they have turned into compliant centrists, the illuminating point is that a triumphant smugness appears to sincerely celebrate the taming of the right and those "embarrassing" people "who founded the Reform Party."[4]

Rarely is the hypocritical symmetry of what is felt by social conservatives within the CPC actually spoken about so honestly. While it is gut-wrenching to think about, it points to an ingrained culture struggling with the awkward tension that must be carefully maintained by the party's faceless internal administration, the grey men and women that define the culture and run things behind the scenes.

The social conservatives are desperately needed by the CPC and resentfully tolerated at the same time. I wonder if this is the unfortunate gilded cage in which the Christian, faith-confessing Leslyn Lewis is kept—is she, perhaps, a visible but subverted moniker sustained to assuage the social conservatives and gaslight them with hope? I ask this question with absolute respect for Ms. Lewis and wonder about the reach of her contributions to Canada if this alleged purpose didn't constrain her.

In case you thought the last seventeen years may have given Mr. Poilievre enough time for more thoughtful circumspection on the value of faith (or people of faith) within the CPC, the recent communication arising out of the visit of the apparently Christian politician Christine Anderson, to Canada, in February 2023, suggests he cares very little about the important nuances that should be holding the party together.[5]

His brutal condemnation of Christine Anderson as being vile, racist, and hateful is all the more difficult to absorb, especially when Ms. Anderson was meeting with three Conservative Party of Canada MPs—including Leslyn Lewis.

Ms. Anderson is a German Member of the European Parliament (MEP) with the German political party called the Alternative-For-Germany Party (AFG), a right-leaning minority party that holds 78 seats in the German Bundestag. The party rose to prominence on a platform to control immigration after Angela Merkel allowed 1.3 million undocumented migrants and refugees into Germany. The AFG appears to distinguish between moderate Muslims, calling them valued members of society, and radical Islam, which does not seem so challenging a distinction when one considers the events since 9/11 and most of the Western nation's foreign policy for the last twenty years. There is much debate about whether the AFG is far right, but it seems that in Germany, what is far-right and populist, is defined by the left-leaning media.

Many have observed Christine Anderson as a consistent international voice for freedom throughout the Covid Pandemic lockdowns and travel restrictions. She has supported and praised the Freedom Convoy, and has repeatedly spoken to the growing causal link between the vaccination and adverse events (and now the actuarial deviations and spike in the new category of death: the died suddenly and unexpected death categories).[6] She also brought a fairly integrated articulation of what appears to be her Christian faith within government into her response to Mr. Poilievre's unfiltered verbal assault towards her.[7]

There is much to learn from this little scuffle with Poilievre. The Ms. Anderson event should not just be allowed to be simply cancelled and forgotten by the CPC until the lessons her short trip to Canada taught us have been fully reflected upon.

Many CPC party members share something disputably close to her articulation of Christian faith and have resonated with her truth-telling on the real issues over the last two and half years. If you are a Catholic or Protestant Christian conservative, you can now guess what Pierre Poilievre likely thinks of your deeply held spiritual views if they get in the way of his calculus for power the way Ms. Anderson was perceived to do.

How ironic is it that Mr. Poilievre, the leader of Canada's Official Opposition, snapped to attention when the Canadian Anti-Hate Network (and others) demanded it and then responded with venom-like hatred to label, condemn, and cancel? What should have been a careful, nation-building response became a barrage that withered his own popular MPs and alienated those who value religious freedom.

The question has to be asked: If you truly value God and the freedom that our nation gives you to value God, how can you co-exist with this condemnation of your value system by the leader of the political party that is supposed to defend and champion your right to hold that view?

It is time for Christians to reconsider the secular and sacred divide they have enabled inside the CPC and in the government. At some point, co-existence with abuse becomes accepting compliance and then, in turn, it becomes denial. If the *Holy Bible*, Matthew 10:33 specifically, means anything to you, there is a clear choice to make. Canada has a conservative party in name only, so it seems there is a place within the party for those who are Christian in name only as well.

Canadians who align with the Christian faith can be forgiven for being confused or may even feel abused in their relationship with the CPC. It is curious how Ms. Anderson was treated, especially when Mr. Poilievre was so happy to invoke the name of the Christian God to bless Canada in his leadership acceptance speech in September 2022.[8] While this contrast is opportunistic, embarrassing and even cringeworthy, it is hard to reconcile the duplicity in the shallow blessing with the heartfelt fervour of his cursing. JT couldn't have done it better.

At least JT doesn't pretend to value God's name as Pierre Poilievre does. Poilievre may learn that invoking God's name may bring undesirable consequences if done to manipulate others.

Value Dissonance within the CPC

Closely held values and the freedom to exercise them are popping up all over Canada. As I write this today, another pastor, Derek Reimer, has been arrested in Calgary for mischief because he protested at an LGBTQ book reading event *for children*, which was on public property.

Unless there is more to this story that we have not heard yet, it appears that Derek Reimer is endeavouring to righteously stand up against the perverted sexualization of our children facilitated, in this case, by the municipal government in Calgary.

Righteous is a powerful word. The *Merriam-Webster* dictionary says it means "morally right or justifiable" and "arising from an outraged sense of justice or morality."[9] We don't use this word much anymore in Canada, but it is time we did because there is right and wrong, good and evil, and light and darkness in this world.

Ezra Levant of Rebel News recently coupled this term together with Christians to advertise the making of a movie about the persecution of righteous gentiles in Canada.[10] He is doing this as a Jew, I believe, recognizing the help offered by Christians in aiding the Jewish people over the years. Levant said, "This documentary will uncover the truth about how the government's response to the pandemic targeted Christians specifically, and why. This pains me very much as a Jew; and just like there were many righteous gentiles who protected Jews when we were persecuted, I feel a special duty to speak up for Christians who are being demonized and even jailed."[11]

Did you automatically think that Derek Reimer was in the wrong when he was arrested? If so, I invite you to reread the third chapter because that knee-jerk assumption used to be generally true—but it is not anymore. Righteousness means 'making the crooked straight' even when it is a morally bent government. This is what is needed in Canada for this nation to not be lost. Governments don't like people of faith because of their belief in an even higher authority than the government.

How will Pierre Poilievre provide a social or political commentary on this value clash in Calgary or the rationale for this pastor's arrest in light of our Charter when he cannot discern his own duplicity? Our current problems in Canada have grown in direct correlation to the increased distance from the values that built this nation. We are set for even more disappointment, decline, and severe difficulty if we believe that money will solve these issues.

So far, we know Pierre Poilievre has a calculator and a hammer; whether he possesses the moral depth or finesse to navigate these kinds of issues is very much another issue. The fact is that these are very relevant value issues for many Canadians, yet no one seems to want to talk about the sanctity of life inside the CPC. The challenge is that there are so many party members that value life and have strong views on the ideology behind exposing children to lewd and pornographic material, sexualizing innocence, pedophilia, medically assisted suicide, the value of life, abortion, euthanasia, or the primacy of parental rights.

Getting these discussions on the policy agenda has been a real challenge. I have observed some politically active Catholic friends engage some of these issues internally within the party, being validated privately for their views but then were passively resisted within the party apparatus until their effort collapsed.

Many Christians believe that a nation is blessed economically and governmentally when the inherent value God places on each individual is protected within a nation's laws. Yet the party's gatekeepers dismiss conversations about abortion or euthanasia because these topics are too difficult at the polls.

The left is always going to win the race to the left. Conservatives that hold any faith values, or no faith, but adhere to more traditional morality, have to ask how long the party can drift to the left in order to get elected before becoming the left. It seems the Conservative Party of Canada is no longer able to meaningfully chart a course to the right when it comes to these important issues. If the party cannot reform itself to advance these issues, how can it honestly represent the interests of those that genuinely value religious freedom?

The CPC seems to think it is enlightened or somehow noble because it has now broken down the point of the partnership in separating the secular and the sacred within the party's operations. While this convergence was the entire point of the partnership with the Reform Party of Canada, it has now proved to be a total dilution of those values that forged the party. The CPC has forgotten this and clearly revealed its shallow understanding of these moral and religious values in its overwhelming contribution to the Conversion Therapy Bill C-4.

Unanimously supported by all Conservative MPs, this legislation clashed with so many faith perspectives on freedom of religion and the parental authority for children that Conservative MPs don't want to talk about it now. Where does leaving morality and values out of the conversation get the people of faith within the CPC? In this case, it will put you in jail for five years if you talk to your children about God's perspective on their identity and biological sex.

Disconnection of the Grassroots

The local MP used to be the trusted aunt or uncle in the community that acted as a funnel for information through the MP to the party or the parliament in Ottawa. Increasingly the MP has become the advocate for the party to shape the perspectives of the grassroots. This inversion makes members feel as though communication, culture, viewpoints, and policy are deployed downwards to them, and their effort to send meaningful communication upward into the party is getting increasingly difficult.

The recent disqualification of Gerrit Van Dorland is another example of the dissonance that exists at the grassroots, especially when a candidate is supportive of pro-life policies and is specifically against abortion. I understand that this candidate was endorsed and supported by Leslyn Lewis and not chosen because Pierre Poilievre had a preferred candidate. The selection committee of the Electoral District Association (EDA) was overruled.

There is little doubt that it was deemed to be safer to run a candidate that would not cause fiscally conservative voters in the riding to slide left, and so the candidate with deeply held views on the termination of in-vitro human life was kept on the shelf. The arrogant implication of the party's logic is that all social conservatives will just vote for the approved candidate anyway because anything is better than a Liberal MP. So, this is how the CPC continues to veer left.

After Erin O'Toole was defeated in the general election in 2021, I understand that there was an internal report commissioned by the CPC to determine what is continually going wrong at national elections. It is my understanding that the document was extensive, but it was not released to the grassroots.

The beginning of the disconnect with the Canadian conservative electorate is self-evident. The fact that Maxime Bernier captured 5% of the national vote with disgruntled CPC voters and newly activated voters should be an obvious clue to an unmet need in the CPC's offering to its grassroots and Canada as a whole. More and more conservatives are waking up to this, even those who became new members following the leadership race in 2022.

The challenge for the People's Party of Canada is that a libertarian-freedom platform is also impotent to engage what Harper described as 'dark moral nihilism' that is deconstructing Canada because it has also been too scared to call dark moral nihilism what it is: evil.

CPC leadership elections followed by National Elections is another challenge to the trust of the grassroots. The strategy to date has been to appeal to the grassroots membership to secure the top chair, and then when there is a national election, the leader steers hard to the left. Apparently, the logic for this left-steer is that the grassroots will forgive their wise leader when they win because they know they also need to appeal to the swing vote on the left to win an election. This repetitive missteer does not build trust. The membership feels this; just ask the good people in Abbotsford, BC.

The Honourable Ed Fast took this gambit to a whole new level, disregarding the aforementioned two-step approach, and just pushed further left by becoming the Western

Canadian Election Chair for Jean Charest's leadership bid for the CPC in 2022.

Jean Charest is a well-known politician who was Canada's representative to Rio De Janeiro in 1992 for the birth of UN Agenda 21 and whose own Sherbrooke constituents removed him from his seat and the Premier's Office in 2012. After this, Mr. Charest went on to work for Huawei, the Chinese Telecommunications Company, supporting 5G service in Canada. One may only speculate how the centre-right folks in Abbotsford really felt about that 'conservative in name only' leadership candidate being nationally supported by their MP. If they were unhappy, they would be unable to do anything meaningful about it because, as the incumbent in the riding, Mr. Fast is eligible to raise the necessary $15,000.00 so his seat cannot be challenged within the constituency in the lead-up to a Federal Election.[12] If the grassroots did want a leadership change, current policies like this one make it very difficult ever to have such a conversation.

Perhaps the policies that impede the grassroots within the CPC are not that big of a deal to you? Or possibly you don't mind the diminishment of the value of the social conservative perspective in its special partnership within the CPC? Maybe you believe Poilievre's erratic and disparaging comments should be overlooked? If so, let's talk about Canada's national security and the need for the diligent guarding of it. This is something all conservatives should care deeply about.

Foreign Interference

As I write this chapter, we are in the midst of a breathtaking national reaction to the foreign interference in the 2019 and 2021 federal elections by China. What is *so amazing* about this is that we were already fully briefed on this threat coming against our nation in 2019/2020. One can understand why JT and his co-workers would wish to overlook this 2019 report, but where has the Canadian Conservative Party been on this topic?

This report is nearly four years old, and we have had three CPC Official Opposition leaders preside over this very information without any meaningful comments; let alone the apoplectic response that we would expect from a Conservative leader seeking power. When this report came out, the Conservative Party MPs should have led the protest and demonstration in front of the parliament buildings. I personally know that there were Conservative MPs aware of the gravity of this report, but their views were ignored. Why?

The report was not hard to find. I watched a summary of it on YouTube in 2020 and was deeply shocked by what was told to the nation. Our government's response was non-existent—silence was also the official response from the CPC and its leadership. Why was there no response from the CPC when this report should have been perceived as a gift? This should have been such an obvious opportunity to be taken advantage of.

Mr. David McGuinty was the chair of the National Security and Intelligence Committee and a Liberal MP who orally presented a 'deep dive' report from 2019, verbally stating that the assessment of the threat to Canada "is best described at Paragraph 189 on Page 77 [of the report]."[13] He went on to verbally note that:

The Committee believes there is ample evidence that Canada is the target of significant and sustained foreign interference activities [by] the PRC, the Russian Federation [and] other states...all seek to exploit the openness of our society and penetrate our fundamental institutions to meet their objectives. They target ethnocultural communities, seek to corrupt the political process, manipulate the media, and attempt to curate debate on post-secondary campuses. Each of these activities pose a significant risk to the rights and freedoms of Canadians and to the country's sovereignty. They are a clear threat to the security of Canada.[14]

Canada is the target of significant and sustained foreign interference activities...these activities pose a significant risk to the rights and the freedoms of Canadians and to our sovereignty. They are a clear threat to the security of Canada.[15]

Canada is the target of significant and sustained foreign interference...that response can be vastly improved... [Our] message to the Government: that things can be improved...it's time to up our game when it comes to foreign interference.[16]

Please take a moment and re-read these paragraphs. Can you believe there was "ample evidence" of "significant and sustained foreign interference" with "significant risk to [Canadians and Canada]," and *nothing* was done or said by the CPC leadership that I can find at the time of the report, or really thereafter![17]

It is bad enough that there is sustained foreign interference, but note that "they seek to corrupt the political process."[18] The target is the political and democratic process! This language could not be more alarming! Our nation needs root and branch reform within our government.

So where was Her Majesty's Loyal Opposition's response to this in 2019, 2020, 2021, and 2022? If there was any response from Mr. Scheer, Mr. O'Toole, or Mr. Poilievre, it was muted and absent until the story broke again in February 2023 concerning Mr. Han Dong, MP.[19] It seems it may now be politically pragmatic for the civically elected leadership of the CPC to respond as this story appears to be sticking and it is now advantageous to come out of the shadows.

As I write this on March 1, 2023, Leslyn Lewis is finally highlighting the pattern of foreign interference in Canada[20]—this definitely wasn't a topic engaged by the candidates that were allowed to advance in the last CPC leadership race in 2022 despite the verbal report released by the Honourable David McGuinty a year earlier. On the same day, Pierre Poilievre tweeted about the cost of rent increasing in Canada by 10%.[21] What a predictable and safe topic to raise in writing via the mass reach of Twitter when the integrity of the electoral process and democracy itself is at stake.[22]

Why wouldn't Pierre Poilievre take advantage of the CSIS whistleblower's career-risking release of information on foreign interference and shout this out to Canadians? Why play it safe and only reference verifiable housing statistics via Twitter's far-reaching platform? That is not a leadership that informs and protects a nation and its people. National security and election integrity are red-line issues in a democracy and should be a gift to any opposition party truly seeking to disrupt or topple a sitting government.

The existence of this 2019 report on foreign interference is such a compelling piece of work, revealing the vulnerability of this nation and the total impotence of the Conservatives as the Loyal Opposition to highlight it, amplify it—or do anything about it. Their entire *raison d'etre* is to protect the lives and livelihoods of hardworking people, to protect our sovereignty, our borders, our democratic process, and our way of life and hold the in-power government to accountability until it finds a way to attain power itself.

The CPC has done *none* of this. The CPC's response is so deficient on this particular front we need to hope it is just incompetence, for it remains to be seen how an accomplice could support JT and his league of supporters any better than the CPC has.

The root problem for both the CPC and Mr. Poilievre is that they appear to believe that the protection of the lives and livelihoods of Canadians starts and stops with the nation's fiscal and monetary policy. This lack of perception and moral shallowness seems to be a kind of blindness that only permits financial policy to be engaged because it is composed of facts. Why just facts? Because facts are verifiable retroactively and, therefore, safe since the media or the opposition cannot easily attack them.

Intelligence and vision are perceiving opportunity, strategy and threats before they are substantiated by history. This is what faith and vision is about. Our nation's problems are not rooted in our finances but in the value framework that will govern. If one cannot perceive threats beyond what is already financially verifiable—one cannot lead.

Bill C-4 is evidence of this. The report on foreign interference is further evidence of this. The Conservative Party of Canada's repeated stalling on advancing policy to protect the vulnerable can only be perceived as a willful compromise, especially when Canada was left with absolutely no laws controlling or impeding abortion after the Conservatives held power.

The unwillingness to interrogate what the reset means or what a post-nation state looks like is further evidence of this blindness.

If we want this horrible slide to the left of the political and value spectrum stopped, the people who can see what is happening and are passionate about their values need to stand up, unite, and vote accordingly so as not to enable this blindness to unwittingly facilitate the destruction of our nation.

I suspect that the depth of planning that has been undertaken to destabilize and deconstruct Canada is only beginning to be revealed. Likewise, the CPC's inability, or unwillingness, to connect the dots of these plans will become an ugly spectacle of arrogance, omission, and a stubborn, narrow-minded focus on finance—while the soul of the nation is being cut out and replaced with a totalitarian Marxist state.

52 Civil Servants

You may have noted in Chapter Three that I alluded to a group of 52 civil servants working in BC to deconstruct and rewrite the values and rationale behind our society and legal systems. This group is described here as a working committee that was incrementally revealed to me by a brave person assigned to it as a committee member by their municipal Mayor.[23] As an elected municipal official, they were assigned to sit on this multi-tiered committee of elected provincial MLAs, municipal councillors, and provincial and federal civil servants from different sectors, including environment, education, and governance (legal).

To say that I was shocked at the existence of such a group is an understatement, and I found myself writing a 'thought paper' to try to trace the logic and record the nuance and philosophical roots of this working committee in order to understand what their work would mean to Canada.

The language of UN Agenda 2030[24] is slippery—it sounds alluring, attractive, and positive, yet when you really look at what the words mean and how they are used, it is anything but positive. You may wish to stop here to read my previously unpublished article so you have context for the comments that follow. The article is called *The Great Reset: The Deconstruction of Canadian Sovereignty* (see Appendix A for the full text).

Following the completion of this analysis article, it found itself in some very interesting places that I cannot discuss here now. As it happened, I did send it to Pierre Poilievre in his role as the Shadow Finance Minister in December 2020 with the belief that he would pick up on the gravity of what was being planned and catalyze someone to *follow the breadcrumbs* in order to examine, if not expose, this agenda and the organization that was facilitating the planning for the death of the Canada we know and love. I didn't care if he was opportunistic about using this information as I felt it needed to be examined officially to protect Canada (see Appendix B for the full letter).

Let's be very clear here, the purpose and intent of this working committee is to tear down our existing nation and rebuild it as a Marxist nation held up by control that brings captivity, via compliance, with Agenda 2030 and fourth-generation information technology, transhumanism, and artificial intelligence—creating a digital net. Now, more than two years down the road from this article, the evidence for this concern is growing in depth and in its cross-referenced proof of policies to limit freedom, silence dissent, remove firearms, silence the press, control the internet, and just control in general.

They cannot truly and fully control a person unless they implement an integrated network of digital identification that cross-links your passport, driver's licence, insurance, medical information, banking, criminal record, and other bio-data. Of course, we welcome user-friendly applications that empower and mobilize us to greater freedom—who wouldn't want an out-of-province doctor to have access to our medical records to care for us in an emergency away from home? It would be hard to find someone who does not appreciate the ease of paying a bill or sending money to a loved one through Interac or electronic banking. Databases that enhance the ability of the police to isolate data and safely respond to incidents with convicted criminals seem like good things to empower.

Did you know that people who are murdered by poison nearly always ingest it because they were tricked by the promise of enjoyment or benefit? This is the lasting lesson of the Trojan Horse.

The challenge for us is that we have to remember that the government and its systems are supposed to be there to serve and support law-abiding citizens, not the other way around. In every equation where the collective good, or safety of the people, is vaunted as an unassailable value, privacy seems to be compromised.

This compromise perpetuates government overreach and the reduction of the citizen to a faceless unit within the collective that the government wishes to make safer. As technology serves us, it must be constrained by clear and stringent back-stops that protect the privacy and liberties of Canadians. A good government may possess power, but it does not mean it has the lawful authority to use that power against its own citizens.

A lust for control fuels the current political class, leaving our privacy undefended across many fronts, especially when it comes to money. There is no better example of your privacy being compromised and your ability to feed your family being impeded than digital-only (non-cash) currencies. Governments love this idea because they can monitor and control how much you spend, on what, where, and when. If you think digital currency is a bulletproof concept, ask our cousins in Dallas, Texas, how they paid for things in the ten days their city was without power in February 2021. It wasn't digital currency, and they weren't using Interac.

When digital currency is coupled with CCTV systems and the encouragement of citizens to snitch on each other, it becomes the building block for total social control. This is the same kind of system China uses as a social-credit system to track and punish its citizens for behaviour deemed to be anti-social.

J-walking, spitting, protesting, and displaying the wrong attitudes (or whatever) don't just generate fines—they may also impact what school your child goes to, whether you get or keep your job, what apartment you live in, or what your interest rate is on your mortgage. Remember who it was that JT admires?

The working committee referenced earlier is apparently designing a shared prosperity index that will be tracked by the government, rewarding citizens that cooperate, charging higher costs for behaviour deemed as unsustainable, and implementing a contemplated mechanism to "remove, or change, those individuals that inhibit progress toward sustainability."[25] That is a direct quotation from their working documents.

We need to wake up; this is 'only' about control.

Christine Lagarde, who is the former Director of the International Monetary Fund (IMF) and is now the Director of the European Central Bank, was pranked and tricked into an interview with Russian pranksters *Vovan and Lexus* because she apparently thought she was speaking with the Ukrainian leader Zelensky on the topic of the Digital Euro. The interview is in English and was recently posted on the Dutch Channel Klokkenluiders; in it, Christine Lagarde said:

> The Digital Euro is going to have a limited amount of control. There will be control, you are right, you are completely right. We are considering whether for very small amounts, you know—anything that is around Euro 300–400—we could have a mechanism where there is zero control, but that could be dangerous.

The terrorist attacks on France, back 10 years ago, were entirely financed by those very small, anonymous credit cards that you can recharge in total anonymity.[26]

Note the language used here. "Zero control" by the government means danger for the safety of the state. The important concept of the privacy of citizens is framed as "total anonymity," which creates an environment where terrorist attacks can lurk.[27]

We used to rely on our intelligence services, military, and police to be the net that disrupted and caught threats before they materialized, ensuring the privacy of the general population until a person came under investigation. Now we can just monitor every citizen and sift all transactions, tracking every citizen with algorithms.

Why is this a bad thing if you have nothing to hide and everyone is kept safer? The argument is so compelling, except that to take this approach, we involuntarily sacrifice privacy and are required to trust the government even more to be the protector and enforcer of our Constitutional rights. This anemic logic might be worthy of debate if we had observed our government to authentically champion the defence of our privacy and our *Charter of Rights and Freedoms*. Our national challenge is that we know that it has not done that.

The truth in Canada is there was no validation or defence of our nation's Charter rights when it came to Covid-19. We were given a new and arbitrary constitution defining what was essential and non-essential in our society. The government tracked our location for compliance with health bylaws. What did the Conservative Party of Canada

MPs say to condemn this violation of the *Canadian Charter of Rights and Freedoms?* How about the imprisonment of the pastors when they held their church services and then were arrested for Covid violations, all while Costco heaved with shoppers? They said nothing.

Our *Constitution and Charter of Rights and Freedoms* are supposed to be what defines an essential service—not unelected, overzealous health officials. It is profoundly troubling that James Coates and Artur Pawlowski were imprisoned for exercising their pastoral leadership of charitable work and feeding the poor. More concerning is how bail conditions appear to further infringe upon Charter rights, which in turn means it appears that any accused person who allows themselves to be arrested when standing up for their Charter rights is asked to consent to bail provisions, requiring them to refrain from the same behaviour that got them arrested. While this requirement is not uncommon and reasonable to stop criminal acts, it poses a real problem if you believe that what you were arrested for was not actually illegal in the first place. If these citizens are principled, they will not sign their bail condition as it is tantamount to pleading guilty to the very thing that got them arrested.

Being arrested should not automatically mean you are incarcerated for weeks or months on end. It is still the law within Canada that you are innocent until you are proven guilty, and the careful test established to permit release on bail and protect the public from repeat offenders is appearing to become politicized.

The process of justice should not be permitted to become the punishment.

The fact that so many charges are now being dropped by the Crown before trial is an indicator of how the law is being trivialized to control and punish rather than ensure that justice prevails. This is the rule by law which is very different from the rule of law established in the preamble of our *Charter of Rights and Freedoms*.

The use of 'mischief' as a *catch-all* criminal charge is another indicator of this trend to arrest and label those who stand up for their rights, neutralize their voice, and control them. We have seen this with the three gentlemen in Coutts, Alberta, who were charged with mischief in September 2022 and seven months after the protest at Coutts was disbanded.[28] These individuals—Alex Van Herk, Marco Van Huigenbos and George Janzen—are now living with the stress of a trial date that keeps moving and is currently set for April 2, 2024.[29]

It can take the RCMP about six minutes to issue a mischief citation and used to be brought against kids that spray-painted messages on buildings and bus stops. Why did it take six months for the three southern Albertans to get arrested? It does not appear that there was any new evidence that came during that waiting period. It is starting to appear that the criminal code is being weaponized and the RCMP politicized—especially where there is an agenda for them to be used to silence those speaking out about the erosion of freedom and the rights that support it. In the scenarios where people are more compliant, the mechanisms for control are more incremental, just like the gradual temperature change for the frogs that slowly boil to death because they don't notice the heat increasing.

The deployment of the plan to create 15-minute cities

erupted very shortly after the Davos meetings in 2023, defining the little paddock for people to live in, incentivizing them not to move, and potentially punishing those who leave. London, England, has an earlier iteration of this as their citizens are punished for entering the city if their mode of transportation does not meet the permitted carbon emissions within the Ultra-Low Emissions Zone (ULEZ).

If you had travelled around London in the 1980s or even the 1990s, you would know that lowering soot and diesel fumes in the city was a good idea—but the challenge arises to our understanding of privacy and free movement when you join all these technologies together and reflect on the government's willingness to disregard long-established rights when they have the ability to do so.

This joining of the technologies creates a potent tool in the hands of the state for control that is becoming as effective as the Berlin Wall—only these are technological bricks. Canadians have already learned the power of the Financial Transactions and Reports Analysis Centre of Canada (FINTRAC) system when coupled with a government that was made to feel insecure by donations to the Freedom Convoy. Bank accounts were frozen, and it was only cash that permitted people who were targeted by the state to feed their families or to move around.

While privacy is one issue, the trend to shift decision-making power for things like health care to unelected bureaucrats outside of Canada, in the United Nations, should intensify our gaze upon what we are giving up as we give the government dashboards that monitor health, wealth, identity, and free movement—all together at the same time.

We must exercise extreme caution and return to foundational lessons about the individual's inalienable rights in our democratic society.

The alternative to individual rights is the *rights of the collective.* JT always seems to refer to this as he stares into the distance, scolding us about what the truly good Canadians think or know. This is the epicentre of the value clash in Canada. Individual rights, family, property ownership and our understanding of wealth are being targeted—labelled as being individualistic and selfish, as revealed by this working committee creating a new social construct for us while deconstructing the Canada we understand and love.

I was staggered at the scope of the planning and the manner by which our entire nation was being conceptually broken up—this would be comparable to the Vimy Ridge monument in France having its beautiful white marble tiles and brick internal structure harvested to build a prison or a barn.

When I looked deeper into this working committee of civil servants, I discovered that this group was convened, and the work was done within a not-for-profit organization funded substantively by large grants from the Liberal Government. In my view, the activity of this group can only be defined as sedition, treason, and conspiracy to commit treason against the people of Canada. I suggested to my contact that if the intentional and repeated meetings over the years were ever analyzed together from a future vantage point looking backward, it might be observed that the actions were so destabilizing that they were actually treasonous. This is what the Nuremberg trials taught us. When an informed value lens is applied retroactively, actions can be seen differently and judged as wrong and even evil. It does not matter if you were only following orders or could lose your job if you didn't obey.

Please allow me to digress here for a moment. This is also why the Hippocratic Oath is so imperative for doctors and other medical professionals because it establishes a personal moral and professional standard of care requiring medical personnel to 'do no harm' and 'ensure there is informed consent' as opposed to coercion.[30] The impulse by the government to control the ethics of the medical profession simply because they pay them may have the intention to neutralize the safeguard of this moral authority entrusted to doctors, which is codified in their oath. In this way, doctors shift from professionals with a fiduciary duty to their patients first to becoming employees of the state, paid to disburse politicized medical treatments.

This oath will be the starting point in the review of our medical system as the mechanism to deliver the experimental Covid-19 vaccine under the emergency use provisions. The evidence of causal links between the point of vaccination and injury (adverse event), or death, must be properly examined. Where there is fraud, medical indemnification needs to be nullified.

We must discern whether there is criminal intention, recklessness, or negligence in the deployment of this untested drug on the Canadian people. The statistical standard deviations being observed by insurance company actuarial tables point to a possible intervening event that may align with a spike in unexpected deaths and 'died suddenlies.' Those that have taken oaths will provide a starting point to assess the fulfilments of the fiduciary obligations owed to citizens across Canada, whether the oath is for elected officials, public servants, the military, or law enforcement personnel.

The email communication between Mr. Poilievre and myself follows after the written piece entitled: *The Great Reset: The Deconstruction of Canadian Sovereignty* (see Appendix A).

The email written to Mr. Poilievre is called: *Multi-tiered intergovernmental shadow committee to support Reset* (see Appendix B).

The point of including this material is first to reveal how subtle and deceptive the specific language is of *Article 2030*, as observed in November 2020, and how the intentions exposed in the working notes of this working committee are now being evidenced as actions currently being implemented throughout Canada. Secondly, this communication from Mr. Poilievre displayed a childlike refocusing on what he wished to be examined when presented with the outline framework for a strategic plan to undermine our nation.

I did not expect him to accept what I was saying at face value without undertaking some due diligence. However, I identified who I was, my political membership and the professional body that I was responsible to (The Law Society of Alberta) as a point of accountability for why I would not present him with a fictional story or send him on a wild goose chase. You may choose to review Mr. Poilievre's email response to me in the Appendix.

In Poilievre's response, he quoted what Justin Trudeau had specifically said by identifying "the facts" and then went on to say, "We need the government to focus instead on protecting the lives and livelihoods of hardworking people."[31] Acknowledging that JT factually said the words 'reset' and 're-imagine,' Poilievre refused to recognize the intention or agenda behind the words or the meaning of the words. The intention, agenda, and meaning behind those words were made to become non-facts by Poilievre with the unspoken message of 'please only look at what we consider to be important for you to think about—money.'

There was a flippant and complete failure on the part of Poilievre to perceive that his reference to the "lives and livelihoods of hard-working people"[32]—Canadians—actually rests upon the democratic framework, our definition of prosperity, and the value system that this group of bureaucrats was deeming to be 'incorrect' and seeking to destroy.

This is akin to saying, 'Let's advance our economic vitality, and don't worry about the erosion of the fabric of our nation.' How long can you advance one at the expense of the other?

The CPC continues to choose not to talk about the reality we are sliding towards. It remains to be seen whether this is some kind of safety-induced political coma enabling the slide, or whether the CPC is complicit in the slide. In light of this, it is easy to understand why some people believe the CPC is simply the 'paid opposition' and that it is the third leg of a uni-party stool, aiding in the unravelling of Canada.

I am asserting that a singular focus of the economy as a safe platform with verifiable data is causing the party, and by extension, Mr. Poilievre, to miss the forest while staring at a single tree. Bill C-4, the 2019 report on foreign interference and the castigation of Christine Anderson are all evidence of this narrow vision and dwarfed moral understanding.

My exposure and analysis document, included in the Appendix and dated 22 November 2020, was seeking to provide Mr. Poilievre with initial and prima facie evidence that Trudeau's working committee of 52 people was actually working every month to "re-imagine" what the country would look like and to "re-set" how it would work.[33] The easy evidence of who was doing it and where it was being done was purposefully withheld by me for a later purpose, but there was not even the simplest inquiry made about my assertions from Mr. Poilievre concerning the work of this group. This was surprising.

My article, *The Great Reset: Deconstruction of Canadian Sovereignty,* found its way to several surprising places.

The first was to the RCMP, which contacted me about this with interest in whether any foreign interference was involved. This was hardly surprising given the 2019 report referenced above, which they must have been very cognizant of.

The second was a cluster of Conservative MPs who received and reviewed the document and were instinctively aware of the existence of philosophical work being done to erode the fabric of the nation but shocked at how developed, organized, and extensive the group who were designing the blueprints of a new nation.

My impression of the handful of Conservative MPs that

received this document was that there was no politically pragmatic channel available at that time to open this matter up or provide any fruitful traction to engage this.

This interface made it very clear that we have a gaping problem with the intelligence membrane of CSIS as an observer and information gatherer passing the enforcement baton to the RCMP, whose mandate is to apply our Criminal Code and other laws. Our political system has clearly not given the RCMP the operational will to investigate and enforce the laws we have, even though they are supposed to be independent. They appear unable to act without the evidence that is only observable *after* the impact of the crime is understood—which is obviously too late. The fact the RCMP is effectively paid by the Federal Government or its agents must impact its independence and paves the way for discussions about it being politicized.

The political apparatus is the leading tool and nervous system, identifying ideological threats to the existence of a nation. In our current circumstances, the Liberal Party of Canada is the perpetrator leaving the CPC as the guard and watchdog against sedition, conspiracy, foreign interference, fiduciary compromise, and treason. All we have heard officially from the CPC on these matters is radio silence. If the CPC had done something internally to thwart this assault on our nation, it was not enough and is now irrelevant. If something had been done about any of these matters, we would have heard it highlighted, the same way we hear about Poilievre successfully challenging the blank-cheque spending of the Liberal Government during Covid.

Let me say that my criticism of this ship called the CPC is not a criticism of all the sailors on it. There are still many good people working within the party, but there seems to be an atmosphere or an invisible hand of influence within the organization, making the collective direction and strategy appear insecure, erratic, compromised, and even stupid—yet, many of the individuals that make up the collective group are clearly brilliant individuals and passionate Canadians.

The bottom line here is that there appears to be an agenda to deconstruct Canada, and it does not matter whether the CPC is choosing not to see it or is blind to it. Either explanation is not acceptable anymore.

The partnership that built this party has been so diluted that it is irrelevant. The social conservative vote is being used to attain power while the moral and religious values that social conservatives care about are filtered, sanitized, and isolated behind the glass of the secular and sacred divide—then they are simply ignored.

The CPC has gone woke, Pierre Poilievre is the current Pied Piper, and Leslyn Lewis is tolerated and kept within the party so that social conservatives don't go elsewhere and split the vote. The fear of splitting the vote is the most potent unifier in the party.

The very painful problem is that CPC lost three elections even though the vote was not split, with the last two specifically because they drifted left and continue to do so.

If the Liberals can undermine and lay the plans to destroy Canada with a minority government, imagine what the social conservatives and Christian right could do to fix it while leading a minority government.

6

CHAPTER SIX

A Polite Intervention: What We Have Forgotten as a Nation Holds the Keys for the Solution We All Need and Want

Our *Charter of Rights and Freedoms* is very clear. Every single section of it starts with the words:

> Whereas Canada is founded upon principles that recognize the supremacy of God and the rule of law:[1]

That is a colon after the word 'law.' In case you haven't thought about it, this colon means that every single provision in the Charter that follows the preamble starts with that preamble to be properly read before each section. We don't tend to read it like that now, and many prefer not to read it like that, hoping that God is just an historical fiction. He is not that.

There is an ancient proverb that says, "Where there is no revelation, people cast off restraint."[2] This is where we are right now in Canada because we have lost the revelation (understanding) of the principles that built this country. Interestingly, this proverb is also written on the west window of the Peace Tower in Ottawa by previous Canadians who thought this was important for us to remember.[3]

Our founders believed in the God of Abraham, Isaac,

and Jacob and built this nation around principles that the country grew up surrounded by. Many of those principles in our Charter are freedoms rooted in the laws of God, which in turn were given in the *Ten Commandments,* and then established in our common law starting with the *Magna Carta* in 1215.[4] Revisionists might not like these facts, but it was on these principles that all of the most successful democratic nations were built. The inherent value of this value system was self-evident even to those who did not believe in God. When these truths are hidden, tyranny takes a foothold, and slavery follows as truth is rewritten.

I have already noted how the further we get away from these values, the more unrecognizable the country looks. Justin Trudeau and his league of supporters are trying to introduce a new set of values to deconstruct the Canada we know. I refer to this agenda by JT as creating *a new social contract.*[5] There are many facets to this which I have touched upon in other chapters, but the most visceral ones are the sexualization of our children and enabling a financial ransoming of our nation—that will cost us our sovereignty if we allow it.

Our children are being exposed to debauched and lurid literature in our schools that normalizes immoral sexuality. This is the loss of innocence and the beginning of incremental grooming of the children in our society toward pedophilia. When you hear the words 'love means love' within the ideology of the progressive left, it means that even pedophilia is acceptable because *all* love should be treated equally. This is why there is a desire to change the language from being labelled as a pedophile to defining this illicit sexual intention as someone who is a minor-attracted person. Pedophile is a word that properly contains the necessary moral judgment it should. Pedophilia is wrong,

A war is raging for the soul and identity of Canada.

will stay wrong, and it will stay a criminal offence. If you mess with our children, you will be met with a clear and lawful response.

If the people don't rise up in response to protect our children, it will be said that we were too weak to keep our nation.

A war is raging for the soul and identity of Canada.

This war is the eternal struggle between light and darkness, freedom and tyranny, and the God-given rights of the individual set against the amorphous will of 'the collective,' slowly setting itself up to create a captivity for the free people of Canada.

In the Second World War, our elders physically fought and died to defeat a belligerent, national socialist enemy that possessed the demonic agenda to subjugate free people and then, through fear and an ideological framework that feigned morality, silenced dissent and 'cleansed' the 'undesirables' from society. Those who threaten our generation and our society seem to have the same idea, but they have simply reversed the strategy and commenced their assault on freedom in Canada by stealthily making the changes in the government first.

This book is not about what darkness does—it is about what we need to do to counter darkness, take back this nation, and restore it to its foundational principles with vigilance against all who threaten it, whether they be foreign or domestic threats. This message is about returning the light to the public square and into our government.

This nation has not only forgotten the principles and values that built it, but we have also forgotten how this nation has been dedicated to God by its founders on both the French and English sides of our history, followed by generations of Canadians since then. It continues to be dedicated to God daily by millions of Canadians.

These past and present prayers of dedication are spiritual markers for truth, justice, and freedom—prayers that seek to make crooked things straight again. These markers are like long spikes driven into the ground or memorial stones that are a testimony to what people are about. They don't just point back to a lost and dead generation, they resonate with sounds that will guide and align our future. They hold and speak to ancient truths that our society seems to have forgotten. They reveal covenantal roots. Darkness prefers these truths stay forgotten, yet they remain, nonetheless, quietly embedded in hearts and hearths across our nation. They have been laid down on this land and will not be easily uprooted by a few years of a ridiculous Liberal Government with profound legitimacy and ethical issues.

Now that people are waking up to the subversion of the free people of Canada by these clandestine agendas of a reset or post-nationalism, these spiritual markers are being activated again by a remnant of people who have not forgotten the God that upholds these founding values.

You don't have to be a person of faith or even believe in God to see that it is worth contending for these demarcating principles of truth, justice, and freedom. Generations of Canadians have already done this for us—in both World Wars and other conflicts around the world.

The leaves of this nation represent the healing of the nations that reflect our mandate for peace.[6] Canada has been established and taken up a mantle as a nation of refuge for the poor, the persecuted and the weak to establish a better life in a place where He (God) shall have dominion from sea to sea, as is stated in our national motto: *A Mari Usque Ad Mare.* I recognize how symbols like this one might be incredibly antagonizing to some who wish to see them airbrushed out of the story of this nation. Still, the fact is that they are an integral part of who we are as a people, and there are countless Canadians who still deeply resonate with these perspectives and may have even come to this nation because of these values for a new start. The purpose of this book is to caution and advise this silent majority, prompting them to contend for these values and make their voices heard so that the unravelling of this country stops now.

Since writing the above paragraph, John Ivison from the *National Post* has written a disturbing article highlighting the Liberal changes to the long-standing symbols of Canada by amending the design of the Canadian Crown that sits on top of the official Canadian coat of arms.[7] This change has also occurred to the front of the passport by removing the religious symbol of the Christian cross and *fleur-de-lis,* replacing them with maple leaves and snowflakes. These changes are incredibly impertinent for a Prime Minister who presides over a minority government, especially when the changes are done without the consultation of the Canadian people. Does it not appear that making secret changes like this reveals an insecure desperation that ironically validates the existence of God?

If you are reading this and don't believe in God, or are frustrated by the discussion of His existence, don't worry. He is not insecure and has generously given you a choice to discern what or who you will worship, even if it is not Him. Interestingly, that is exactly what *freedom of religion* means to all Canadians.

The markings of this dedication of Canada as a nation under God's dominion and blessing are written all across our history, our families' histories, our laws, and our monuments. Many of the quotations I have referenced throughout this book are written into the very stones, glass, and brass of our parliament buildings.[8] There is providential energy and power to these inscribed truths that should not be underestimated as they are re-activated by the remnant of the faithful who understand the source and the intention of God's purpose in our foundations.

We must not think that because many collectively forgot that God has a dedicated purpose for Canada as a force for good in this world, that God forgot his purposes in this nation.

The link between spiritual faith and the government was wisely identified by Archbishop Fulton J. Sheen in 1947. He said:

> A nation always gets the kind of politicians it deserves. If a time ever comes when the religious Jews, Protestants and Catholics ever have to suffer under a totalitarian

state, which would deny to them the right to worship God according to the light of their conscience, it will be because for years they thought it made no difference what kind of people represented them in Congress, and because they abandoned the spiritual in the realm of the temporal.[9]

Perhaps we have not arrived at a totalitarian state yet, but in March of 2023, the United Kingdom passed the first *thought* crime legislation designed to stop people silently praying in the proximity of abortion clinics in England and Wales.[10] The agenda is to criminalize any 'influence' near an abortion clinic. The legislation was drafted and enacted to deal with a Christian woman in the UK for simply standing across the street outside an abortion clinic. She was not even protesting—just silently praying. The police asked her what she was doing there, and when she said she was praying, the legislation followed.

The application of this UK legislation to create buffer zones is strikingly similar to the approach taken by Calgary Mayor Jyoti Gondek's bylaw that prevents people from protesting within 100 meters of public libraries where drag queens read sexually suggestive and explicit material to young children.[11]

Canada has not yet arrived at full-blown thought crimes, but the way is now paved, and the speed and direction of travel are unmistakable. We are only inches from Archbishop Sheen's understanding of a totalitarian state in Canada.

Religious Freedom in Canada?

When will the Jews, Protestants, Catholics and other

religious persons aggregate around a political agenda to actively preserve religious freedom in Canada?

I found an article I had saved from the *National Post*, dated October 21, 2011, by Charles Lewis.[12] The article discussed the launch of the 2011 Tory promise to open an office of religious freedom to monitor and report on abuses of religious freedom around the world. It discussed the correlative link in society between religious freedom, democracy, and economic stability in the developing world. I have observed this powerful link to be true in places where no governmental corruption overrides the truth of this synergy.

In 2023, the Tories unanimously supported and helped pass laws to stop all Canadians from talking about their religious views of a God-given identity with their children in the privacy of their own homes (Conversion Therapy Bill C-4) and the leader of the Conservative Party of Canada, Mr. Pierre Poilievre, called a Christian politician 'vile' and in another circumstance allegedly blocked a conservative 'pro-life' candidate in Oxford, Ontario from competing in by-elections. Poilievre has only been in office since September 2022. How far has the Conservative Party of Canada come in 12 years?

The irony is that the entire intention of the new Ambassador of Religious Freedom was to protect persecuted minorities *outside of Canada*, citing Egypt and China as examples. "Tom Flanagan, a former advisor to Stephen Harper and professor of political science at the University of Calgary," was quoted in that article saying that the Conservative Party's promise of this new role for religious freedom was "good policy as well as good politics."[13]

If the 2011 Conservative Party logic that "democracy can never work without religious freedom," which in turn enables "economic stability," holds true for developing countries[14]—it is hard to imagine why that would not be true within the party now.

Religious freedom does fortify democracy, and stronger democratic processes do enable economic security. Stephen Harper was right, and so was Tom Flanagan. The fact this logic has been lost or is even being questioned in these 12 years within the Conservative Party should have alarm bells ringing for the membership of the Conservative Party of Canada, demanding an explanation for these incongruencies from the party. At best, this exemplifies shocking philosophical incompetence; at worst, it reveals a policy change by osmosis.

How do you advocate for religious freedom in the developing world on such solid logic and then subvert it in your own country? The inevitable answer is that this version of the Conservative Party of Canada no longer truly values religious freedom.

There are now serious questions about the ability of our national institutions to protect religious freedom and other liberties that have been firmly established in our Charter. Yet for the last eight years, this general responsibility has fallen on the Conservative Party of Canada as the Loyal Opposition, and their response has been muted and inadequate, contributing to the erosion by their omission to champion our Charter freedoms.

This creates a serious quandary for religious people and those who may be classified as God-fearers, meaning they adhere to some notion of a divine creator but are not fervent parishioners of any particular faith. Religious freedom is a core value for Canada and a non-negotiable for many Canadians of faith, and those with no faith, who are within the Conservative Party of Canada.

There is a *quid pro quo* to every relationship of convenience where each party in a relationship gives something to get something. The longer the relationship exists, the longer it takes to recognize that something is broken after the functional relationship stops working. This is especially true in relationships where there is geographical remoteness along with the everyday demands in the lives of citizens. It takes time for a group of individuals, spread across a country like Canada, to understand that a deal-breaking shift of value has occurred, then galvanize a collective response to engage with and then fix it.

Where there is abuse, it often takes the victim longer to realize that the relationship has deteriorated. Perhaps there is a distraction, denial, or low self-esteem, which causes the victim to endure longer in the relationship. This is especially true when gaslighting and carefully planned gestures induce the victim to hope that things will auto-correct. An example of this kind of manipulation is Mr. Poilievre's carefully planted references invoking the name of God during his leadership acceptance speech in September 2022 and many times since.

At some point, either the victim will leave the relationship or someone else will launch an intervention to wake them up to their inherent value, thereby interrupting the pattern of abuse, creating a space for the victim to realize how they have been treated and that they no longer need to be disparaged, de-valued, or treated like crap.

Consider this a political intervention if you will receive it.

I have discussed what this nation has been founded upon and how we are drifting away from our moorings without considering what we are drifting toward. There are many faiths in Canada, and each has a body of principles that establishes a value system, providing a common reference point for us as Canadians. We value the authority of parents to protect our children, and we don't want the government interfering in our worship. It is for others to comment on the nuances of these many faiths and how they relate to our society, but I can comment on the core views of the Christian faith. With 53.3% of Canadians saying they are Christian,[15] I ask again—why is the Christian voice in Canada absent from the public square?

7

CHAPTER SEVEN

Where in This Hell Is the Christian Church?

This chapter is addressed specifically to the Christian church in Canada in 2023.

The *Holy Bible* teaches that "faith without works is dead,"[1] that the Lord and Saviour, Jesus Christ, has instructed you that "as you go," you are to bring His kingdom of light, love, and forgiveness with His power,[2] discipling nations[3]—especially the one in which you reside. You are well aware of what causes a nation to be secure and elevated, and you teach that "where the Spirit of the Lord is, there is freedom."[4]

This nation was left as a legacy for all Canadians, with God's name written across its granite, glass, brass, and coat of arms. Still, the church went into the plushness of its buildings, creating an insulated subculture, and established an annual pilgrimage of compliance that culminates in the annual signing of its T3010 for Revenue Canada.[5] We are here now in this troubling condition because the Christian church failed to be a catalyzing voice shaping Canada with God's principles and laws, as past generations had.

The all-powerful charitable tax receipt, designed to incentivize charitable giving, has become a constraint in the tug-o-war played out across the country between governing boards obsessing about their legal fiduciary obligations and with ministry leaders and pastors feeling fettered in their calling because of compliance issues where the CRA must be satisfied first.[6] Many charities did very well with the Canadian emergency response funds,[7] and the regulatory boards loved it. Compliance with the lockdown was not an issue for them as their staff were happily *locked away*, while some charities and churches were able to significantly enhance their balance sheets.[8]

The red-letter instruction in Matthew 10 to *wash the lepers* sets a pretty high standard for how God's disciples are to respond during a pandemic.[9] The contemporary church left that space a long time ago, at least in regard to how it functions in North America.

It seems many have now abandoned the spiritual in the realm of the temporal, as foreseen by Archbishop Fulton J. Sheen.[10] You have permitted darkness to define light in our public square. You have allowed the secular to demarcate your sacred place in society. You have let the potency of your spiritual salt and yeast be reserved for reviving individual souls rather than reforming society. You have engaged half the Gospel—comfortable with preaching as established in Mark 16:15 but, in most cases, neglecting the call in Matthew 28:19. Church growth statistics are flat, if not shrinking, except for the strong emergence of churches built around Canada's many new cultural immigrant communities.[11]

Until Jesus returns, the mandate still remains to be salt, light, and yeast.[12] The call for every believer in Christ is to reveal transformative love and influence, shape, and orientate your nation toward truth, justice, forgiveness, peace, and thriving fruitfulness. The Christian church in Canada has missed the mark when it comes to pollinating government policy or national direction. It slept. It accommodated. It compromised. It allowed a lot of wrongs to happen because the silent majority thought the country could absorb it all and still be ok. You have been led into a cul-de-sac with the Conservative Party of Canada dangling the promise of punching a road through for your values, but it hasn't followed through—and it won't.

You actively teach that God has no grandchildren, yet rely on the legacy of actions from other generations of people of faith in the public square in Canada to be your covering when you have failed to stand. Some churches are already apostate, and some need to be reminded of what their salt is supposed to do to an infected wound before it can heal. Many are awakening to understand what Jesus Christ, the Lord and Saviour, meant in using the Roman word *ecclesia,* bringing awareness to the application of His influence in society and the government of His kingdom.

Some of these last types of churches seem to exist now. They are increasingly being identified as those churches that truly see themselves as essential and are growing increasingly uncomfortable with trying to serve two masters, especially when the government is now clearly taking positions on morality that violate scriptural truth. I know of a few churches that have decided to stand, including one in Edmonton, Alberta, and others across the nation, now reassessing the new context for their ministry—asking themselves how long they can pause and waffle around between two opinions.

This is no small problem for your leaders, who at some point will be confronted with making a decision about whether God came first with His eternal purpose, rights, principles, freedoms, norms, and mores, or the Canadian government with the CRA and their health bylaws.

This is exactly why I wrote Chapter Six, highlighting the importance of the preamble within the *Canadian Charter of Rights and Freedoms*. This is precisely where the *Constitution of Canada* intersects with the role and responsibility of the Christian church in Canada. The priorities have already been determined and codified. The fact they have been compromised and diluted does not mean these foundation stones have been removed, neutralized, nullified, or deemed irrelevant. The situation can be fixed by simply requiring the will of the people to activate them again, refreshing and mobilizing the people who are empowered to do so. These foundation stones are covenantal to our nation.

This is a thorny issue because identity is the root of much of this discussion. If the Christian church really believes that men and women are created in God's image, are to be fruitful and build families, bring order to the earth, and restore broken relationships, they will have increasing challenges with a government bent towards disorder, deconstruction, or chaos.

Disorder here means the undermining of the family, the disempowerment of parental authority, the destruction of innocence, identity, and self-worth, the subjugation of faith and the Christian faith in particular, and a blood-lust to destroy human life in the womb and actively, before natural death, with euthanasia. Light and darkness do not coexist—except at the point where the shields clash.

Look where turtling has led us; from my understanding of the Scriptures, cowardice comes with a very expensive price tag. It is time to be counted and rise up to what you are called to. Run the race to win, overcome, don't shrink, be brave and courageous, stand, contend, enter, search, expose darkness, shake off the dust, restore what was lost, disciple nations, and be the *ecclesia* in the public square. Remember, 53.3% of Canadians report belonging to the Christian faith. So, what is the impact of this Christian demographic, or more specifically, the Christian church, on how Canada is now governed?

The nation of Canada has never been in more darkness with less truth, justice, and freedom than now. We are less secure and more downtrodden as a nation than ever. We have the unfettered killing of full-term babies in Canada. We have euthanasia. We have Christian politicians being called vile and racist by the leader of the political party in which many Christians have their memberships! We have pastors afraid to preach in pulpits on what is right or wrong or what sin is. We have parents afraid to talk to their children about the abstraction of gender as opposed to biological sex. We have pastors being arrested for rightly protesting against reading sexually explicit material to children in public libraries. We have substantive foreign interference in our election process, and now it appears that our country is being undermined and sold out, forfeiting our people, our way of life, our freedoms, and very possibly our nation as a ransom for the debt we have.[13]

I believe the God of Abraham, Isaac, and Jacob—the God who is Truth and Justice, is offended by the state of affairs in Canada. What is supposed to be His glorious Christian church is caged, mostly impotent and now essentially irrelevant, without even the need for a lock on the cage.

I have read Jesus' teaching in Matthew 16:18, which says that the gates of hell will not prevail against His church. It seems the point of this teaching is that hell is supposed to get pushed back by His church advancing, not the other way around. If I have got the theology wrong here, please let me know.

Yet in every sector of our society, it looks like the gates of hell are prevailing, and the church is virtually absent, forfeiting its place as an advocate for light, truth, justice, and freedom in education, government, media, the arts and entertainment, business, family, and religion. You might argue that the church operates freely in the religious sector—I say it is a leash-wearing, oft-shorn, declawed cat. The gates of hell are clearly here now.

So, let me ask the question again. Where in this hell is the church?

It is not about your buildings. Every single Christian is the church. Is this not what you teach?

Can you honestly hold your Christian values and remain a member of a political party that does not represent them, passes laws that intentionally undermine them, or reserves some of its most vehement hatred toward other Christians who share the same faith and values as you? The time for sitting on the fence of inactivity and indecision as both a citizen and a Christian is over in Canada.

Why is Canada in this decline at all if 53.3% of Canadians who share values from the Christian tradition don't wish the nation to be in decline? The answer rests on the church in Canada and how it has failed to make its faith message relevant and cannot stand with any united purpose. We have been culturally taught to separate personal values from public discussions and join or vote for a political party with economic, health, and energy policies we like or don't like.

You can't talk about the value issues that you base your perspectives on because we have a policy in Canada that requires that you split yourself in two. This bifurcation has silenced Christians and people of all different faiths and allowed family and nation-destroying darkness to advance under a banner of secularism, darkness, moral nihilism, or evil. This is why people of faith, and Christians in particular, are spread all across the political spectrum and feel as though they need to artificially place their value system in the deep freezer of irrelevance to be eligible to comment on important matters in the national political discussion without any moral authority to influence the conversation. This is how we end up with legislation sending parents to jail for having conversations with their children about the sexual identity they were given at birth.

The truth is that while Christians built bigger buildings away from the public square, the secularists discipled our nation and our laws. Good people within the church didn't want to seem unkind, rude, or have some of these difficult conversations in the public square, loving to talk about God's love and grace but forgetting the truth in John 1:14. You teach about grace as God's unmerited favour for His creation but often forget to talk about why it is needed, along with truth, and justice.

Truth precedes justice, and when established, forgiveness,

healing, closure, and health can occur should one choose it. Is this not the message of the Gospel revealed through the person of Jesus Christ? This is basically the same for a nation: truth prepares the way for justice, justice opens the door for forgiveness, and forgiveness creates a pathway for healing and unity should we embrace it. Where should this repentant embrace be modelled or start in Canada?

"How can we heal with zero justice?"

Telegram is such an interesting medium for communication, allowing you to observe and listen to other Canadians whom you may not ever connect with normally, who would not be within your own community or the echo chambers that we can unwittingly create for ourselves online.

There is a man in Canada, who we will call Bob, that administers a private Telegram channel that I have followed since January 2022. He posts a lot, and I find him very interesting as he is both brutally cynical and also hopeful, an aspiring polymath commenting on a diversity of current topics relevant to us in Canada and beyond. Bob is consistently searching for something: the real story, the truth, sharing philosophical thought constructs to explain why we are here and the condition of the human soul. His thought journey is just as engaging as some of the material he posts. I may not agree with everything he shares, sometimes none of it, but he

> *The truth is that while Christians built bigger buildings away from the public square, the secularists discipled our nation and our laws.*

made an interesting post this morning (March 24, 2023).

He posted an informational e-brochure of an upcoming meeting in Surrey, BC, with the headline 'Let the Healing Begin' with photos of all the speakers, academics, and pastors featured at this event sponsored by Laura Lynn Tyler Thompson. For the record, in no way should my comments here be construed as a criticism of Laura Lynn Tyler Thompson or what she is doing for Canada. I have heard her speak. She is a truth-teller and has done a lot to help people to open their eyes to what is happening in our country.

The event brochure appeared to be triggering to Bob, so I won't share his comments here, except for one. After his full rant about healing not being what the country needs, he returned a few minutes later with another singular post written as though he was in frustrated desperation. He simply asked, "How can we heal with zero justice?".[14] This is a great question, and I believe this is the heart cry of the people of Canada right now. They know they have been lied to and manipulated, losing jobs and businesses from policies that violate our very Constitution and Charter. They are broken.

Having watched our elderly die alone behind glass, they are now coming to terms with adverse reactions and many unexpected deaths possibly linked to medication that bypassed the normal process of drug trials. Doctors who saved the lives of dying patients by treating them with established medicines at a nominal cost lost their medical licences. The truth is woefully absent for many of these issues, and the stones have yet to be turned over. Canada needs truth on many fronts because the people of Canada are wounded, disillusioned and broken-hearted, with a sense of our decent upright society crumbling.

Our nation does need to heal stronger and join together in unity once again. This will begin when you relaunch the truth that flows from this nation's understanding of the supremacy of God in Canada. You are the people that bear testimony to this formational truth. Make no mistake, the desire to sully it, hide it, and erase it is a strategic non-negotiable for darkness to be able to prevail.

We can become 'one people, one blood, and one nation' if we use this opportunity to unleash truth, see justice done, and finish the forging of Canada as an independent nation unfettered by the historical tethers still rooted in our colonial past. This is the Canada that I long for.

Canada requires an activated church as one of the stakeholders in our society to wake itself up, stand up against deceit and darkness, and contribute to the building of the nation that you were set in to serve and care for because you are uniquely equipped to respond to evil.

This will happen as you make your presence known again, re-enter the public square with a voice to the government in this nation, and stop allowing your sound to be muffled and neutralized inside political parties that do not recognize the power of your mandate.

Canada is burning. You can help stop it *if* you revive, repair, and rebuild.

Revive means to wake up and act. Repair means stopping the immediate threat and fixing the damage. Rebuild means examining why the fire happened and correcting the systems that failed, ensuring this does not happen again. We need to do these things.

We need only to start by coming together around one value: *Freedom as a gift that has been given.* Then we will recognize that we also share common perspectives on the value of family, freedom of religion, protecting our children, and many other policies that currently need to be addressed in our nation—this is the context and the avenue to re-engage, influence, and shape the public square.

Unless people who share these values unite, mobilizing to contend for Canada in both the spiritual and physical realms, it will continue to advance with its unravelling and decline. The Christian church simply needs to find a way to unite, standing upon the foundational values that built this nation and making them relevant again and felt in the public square.

This will require a new response from the Christian church in Canada, so the gates of hell will no longer prevail here. The definition of insanity is continuing to do the same thing and expecting a different response.[15] We need to provide a strategic change of response, together as one body with many parts.[16] It is not my mandate here to comment further on how this should happen, but my impression is that it is happening already in small, fresh, and different ways across Canada and other nations like the United States and the United Kingdom. There is little doubt that there will be a course correction in our nation as these groups congeal together with other groups in Canada that also stand for the freedom of the human soul.

Chapter Eight

Convoy Conservatives. What Are the Convoy Conservatives? And Why This Group May Catalyze Canada's Grassroot Conservative Renaissance

Even though it appears the term Convoy Conservative was deployed as a subconscious condescension by Tasha Kheiriddin, it actually has the unanticipated quality of opening up a space to have a conversation about this much-talked-about group.

The simple fact is that *irrelevant* things are rarely given special names. No one identifies the lever on their oven as the 'nascent nob that is frequently used in anticipation of dinner' or calls their printer cable 'Gutenberg's silver necklace.' So, when groups of people are tagged with names like the Convoy Conservatives, it generally reveals more about the speaker, or their particular tribe, than it does the newly christened group. It just seems that the purposeful naming of this group somehow points to a correlation with the level of insecurity, fear, or possibly that freshly tagged group's ability to disrupt the established order.

The established order is precious to central Canada.

Like Gollum, in the *Lord of the Rings*,[1] the established order lusts after the ring that secures its longevity and power. This ring is the control and money that is derived from the benefits of an aged electoral process and a policy framework that favours Ottawa, Toronto, and Montreal while population growth and wealth distribution are now more dispersed. Just as Gollum became hysterical when the possession of the ring was threatened or lost, so does the established order obsess about its power shifting away.

In this way, the Convoy Conservatives are first an embodiment of these fears because they generally threaten the established order in Canada and the Conservative Party of Canada, specifically.

Many Canadians who may well fit into this new category do not now discern a difference between Canada's general political direction and the policies of the Conservative Party. Increasingly, they are beginning to see this established order and the Conservative Party of Canada as a uni-party, or two different wings of the same bird, along with the Liberals.

The potency of the threat of the Convoy Conservative is that they have not yet synthesized into a movement, making their political application of force if they do coalesce into this something that can only be predicted. This is why Poilievre has Stephen Harper calling to them and Kheiriddin naming them, as outlined in Chapter Two.

The 'established order' is right to be concerned. Western Canadian alienation, the forcefulness of a militant leftist ideology, and a basket of other live issues currently manifesting within Canada and this cadre of people may just provide the necessary fusion to shatter the prevailing hegemonic order of things. In other words, these people could be game-changers in Canada and even provide the tipping point for a new nation of Western Canada once they get rolling. This is not a hollow supposition.

The real issues the Convoy Conservatives care about...

We are talking about matters of home and hearth, the things that people anxiously share around the dinner table and wake up worrying about in the middle of the night. Freedom is an *essential* part of life, as is religious freedom, the value of family in society, and the parental authority to protect our children and guard their innocence—the bedrock matters of the nation.

After the convoy arrived in Ottawa and before it was vilified and deemed to be 'an occupation,' I watched a recording of a private press conference where Tamara Lich, Benjamin Dichter, and Chris Barber facilitated a conversation on what the convoy was about.[2] I took notes on that press conference because Lich's words that day revealed some of the heart of what the convoy was about; quiet things often reveal truths that are hard to hear.

I listened very closely to what Tamara Lich had to say that day in late January 2022 as she spoke of hope and how proud she was to be a Canadian. Lich made it very clear that she wanted to see unity in Canada and "the veils that hide the problems" disappear in our nation so that we can "heal together."[3] She brought the challenges of a clan mother in Gift Lake, Northwest Territories, who still has no running water. She explained that trust is broken and vulnerability persists, leaving women and families unprotected when issues like this are unresolved, especially following repeated promises to provide water.

Lich was not commenting on our nation as a sociologist or a politician would. This momma bear spoke from the heart of a mother, a grandmother, and a matriarch who wants the best for all of those within her care. While her instinct was to fix what was broken, she could see that betrayal and injustice were getting in the way and that things weren't working; the brokenness was enabling the insecurity and pain of this clan mother's situation.

Beneath the cheers and honking horns, there was a quiet voice of the convoy revealed, calling for truth through the removal of veils, justice in recognition of betrayal (and the actual installation of a water system), unity in a strengthened community where the family and the vulnerable are protected and the healing that inevitably follows when we get real and do the right thing in society.

Remember Telegram Bob, who asked: "How can we heal if we have zero justice?"[4] Lich is asking us the exact same question.

We will be a shallow and weak nation if we ignore these questions and disparage those who risk asking them. The images of Tamara Lich in shackles are simply disgusting, and we should feel shame as a nation for this. The convoy was about Canadian values that our governments were not respecting; these values are buried deep within us. We know it in our bones when our values have been violated, and it doesn't matter that the Supreme Court explains it away or that we can't find the words ourselves to explain how they are violated—we just know something is not right.

Convoy Conservatives know this to be true, acknowledging something is very wrong between the gaps created by what we know and what we are told.

The convoy was about Canadian values that our governments were not respecting; these values are buried deep within us.

We are talking about the fact that our laws are now very uncertain, and our society is unequal. We are talking about the integrity of our democratic process and the sovereignty, security, and enduring health of our people and our nation.

This entire conversation now is about the values of our nation.

It is about the values that built Canada, the values that Canadian soldiers died for, the values we have grown up with in Canada, the values that the 68% of Canadians that call themselves religious, and most everyone else, derive their security, prosperity, and freedom from. We aren't perfect, and we still have some problems to care for in our country, but if we get these ground-zero issues right, we will have a strong foundation to continue building trust on, putting the past properly in the past.

Stephen Harper identified the root of these problems facing Canada 20 years ago. I suspect that political pragmatism and the absence of certain evidence at that time may have curtailed his impulse to tackle and neutralize this threat, but he definitely saw it coming. In his 'Civitas' speech in 2003, as reported by Paul Wells,

Harper said,

> "Conservatives need to reassess our understanding of the modern Left. It has moved beyond old socialistic morality or even moral relativism to something much darker. It has become a moral nihilism—the rejection of any tradition or convention of morality, a post-Marxism with deep resentments, even hatreds of the norms of free and democratic western civilization...
>
> It is a rebellion against all forms of social norm and moral tradition in every aspect of life. The logical end of this thinking is the actual banning of conservative views, which some legislators and 'rights' commissions openly contemplate...
>
> In this environment, serious conservative parties simply cannot shy away from values questions...
>
> On a wide range of public-policy questions—including foreign affairs and defence, criminal justice and corrections, family and child care, and health care and social services—social values are increasingly the really big issues."[5]

If only our problem was that we were too shy! We are now in the very rebellious environment that Harper foresaw in 2003, and yet, we do not have a serious conservative party prepared to deal with social values or the really big issues that flow out of them.

We need to finish the waking-up process that the convoy began. We need to reframe this discussion and realize that the Convoy Conservatives are a gift to this nation because they still carry the same torch from the original fire that forged this nation, illuminating freedom, prosperity, security, truth, justice, human dignity, and the absolute accountability of the government to the people—not the other way around.

They are the canary in the coal mine that will be recorded in our history as the people who drew the first line to stop the deconstruction of the country called Canada, and they will catalyze a serious response to the threats facing this nation now.

This is a battle for the soul of this nation.

So, who are these populists that Harper wants to bring into the Conservative Party of Canada, referred to disparagingly as the Convoy Conservatives? Their DNA is found in the expression of the Freedom Convoy before the media attempted to vilify it and is found in portions of many Canadians who may not have connected all the dots to what is happening yet. Perhaps, these people have just been too timid to say it out loud and shape it into a political platform.

The convoy was an eruption. It was powerful—and an unnerving event to many people in both a good and an anxiety-inducing, disruptive sense. Many people in Canada were delighted to realize that they were not the only ones who 'had enough,' finding fellowship, community, and solidarity in standing up to a government that went too far, wasn't listening, and refused to talk about it.

The Freedom Convoy was about unity. It had people of all colours, creeds, and faiths from all over the nation, including Quebecers, who seemed to feel strong solidarity with other Canadians for the first time in their individual lives. Perhaps this last comment is shocking to you? I know this is true because I have spoken to many of my French-Canadian brothers about the impact of those days and how they felt a connection as Canadians, not just Quebecers who live in Canada. The energy of the event in the early days was almost palpable; some even felt there was a spiritual component to it.

The Canadian Veterans and Diagalon.

I will never forget watching the Canadian veterans remove a wire construction barrier aggravatingly put up to fence off the National War Memorial near the Grave of the Unknown Soldier from the convoy crowds that included the veterans.

It was so insulting to infer that this monument needed to be shielded from the living brothers-in-arms of those men and women who were commemorated in Confederation Square. After the veterans removed this wire fence, the veterans listened to a message from a military chaplain right beside the memorial, sang *O Canada*, and prayed for the country.

One younger veteran, who has now attained some notoriety, recorded his reflections on that particular day as he was walking away from the monument. He said "that it was such an amazing day, that there was something spiritual about it," and that he was "f**king gonna find out what it was," or something very close to that.[6]

I was never able to locate that clip again on social media but learned afterwards that it was Jeremy McKenzie, who a few weeks later crafted the meme about Diagalon, which

I understand was cited to justify the invocation of the Emergency Powers legislation within the Senate.

In case you didn't know it, Diagalon appeared to start as a joke about a fictitious nation that, if it had been specifically explained, was made up of non-woke, meat-eating, gun-owning, God-fearing, pick-up-driving, right-wing, heterosexual redneck conservatives that reside on a diagonal line between Alaska and Florida. This line crossed and included all of Western Canada and was made up of all the 'red' US states.

Some of the best jokes are funny because there is an element of truth to them. I think Diagalon was insightfully designed to tease the hypersensitive, virtue-signalling 'left' with their own worst fears.

Their worst fears might look like an entire nation where the men in it grew up in schools where you got a blue ribbon if you actually defeated the other boys the same age in a competition of strength, endurance, or speed, and it was very seriously contested in the annual primary school sports days. Not everyone got ribbons in those days in Canada, but everyone that earnestly competed was valued for trying their best.

These kinds of boys grew up where teams were picked by playground captains, and you had to earn the right not to be picked last. When there were disputes, they got settled after school, on the ice, or after Rugby practice, possibly even during. These occasional fights were generally short, and sometimes there was blood, but they got things sorted out, often resulting in new friendships. These boys grew up into men that now seem to be resented in our society by a loud

119

minority that like playing their victim card and provoking fights when they can easily escape, just like they learned to do by running to the principal or on-duty teachers during lunch breaks when they were in school.

This is not a homage to testosterone-soaked masculinity but an anecdotal explanation of why this joke would have been funny to some and not to others. It highlights the fact that as much as these virtue-signallers would love to have a world where they get to make unequal rules, Diagalon reminded them there just might be another conception of society where the laws were equal and some who felt safe enough in the protection of those laws to enforce them themselves once they decided to.

If I ever meet Mr. McKenzie, I would like to thank him for this allegory and ask him if my interpretation of the joke about the Diagonalese was right.

Discrimination in Canada?

Canada used to be about equal opportunity. Somewhere along the line, it became about a 'levelling-up' that put certain people further and further away from, and behind, the race's start line. In the 1980s, it was called affirmative action, the United Kingdom called it positive discrimination, and it has been called a host of other names along the way to where it is now known as equitable discrimination.

Equitable discrimination is actually a thing in Canada now, as Queen's University Law Professor Bruce Pardy, in his review of a recent Human Rights Tribunal ruling, made the very poignant point that: "It is time to say the other quiet part out loud: Canadians have not agreed to be treated unequally."[7] This case highlighted that the Human Rights Tribunal had established that white people could not claim discrimination.

If you think this equitable discrimination discussion is only in some obscure Human Rights Tribunal with little application to your life, you will find that it is also brazenly appearing in your local communities, especially if you live in Hamilton-Wentworth or the Waterloo Region in Ontario.

The Hamilton-Wentworth District School Board recently announced that it is having a "Celebration of Belonging" party on May 30, 2023, that restricts the attendance of white staff.[8] The Waterloo Region District School Board held a "career fair restricted to non-white people" on March 29, 2023.[9] Jonathan Kay, a former *National Post* and now freelance journalist, commented on the Hamilton-Wentworth's celebration of belonging party, saying on Twitter, "Because nothing says 'belonging' like segregating events by skin colour."[10]

A lot of Canadians now see this kind of inequity as injustice—period. They also feel the marginalization of sons, brothers, husbands, and fathers because social engineering means they start behind the line.

We know that the marginalization of specific groups like this has been extensively engaged by other commentators. At this particular juncture, my agenda is to try and illuminate some of the lenses through which the 'Conservative Convoy' people see through.

The point here is that the group of Convoy Conservatives are hard-working women and men who do actually exist within Canada; they have families, and they are from multiple faiths and no faiths. It is just that they can't easily be profiled yet because Tasha Kheiriddin's type doesn't know how to isolate them easily or dog-whistle them in for an interview.

If these people were to be contacted by pollsters, many of them might just be too polite to ask the awkward question of the pollster: why are they wasting their time doing a poll when the pollsters got it so wrong in the United States in 2016? They are not necessarily Trump lovers; they just observed that it is possible for digital analysts to not understand the pulse of a people and that the polls don't really tell the full story.

They are not insensitive misogynists like I dramatized the Diagalonese to be, but they likely identify with some of the descriptors I used to profile Diagalon. They don't need to be defended per se—the inequity of their existence needs to be identified to understand why they got named by Kheiriddin in the first place.

There are two types of these people.

The first group has already left the Conservative Party of Canada. I know this is true because there are people who contact me from across the country, telling me they are cancelling their memberships or letting them lapse because they see how the CPC is fighting the wrong battle in the shallow end of the pool.

The second group is still within the CPC and is in various stages of 'waking up' to the awareness of the deeper issues not being engaged by the party. They may not have fully connected the dots yet to see the value decisions that are being made in Canada, making them an outsider in their own country, while being instinctively aware that things are going sideways.

There are a lot of sleep-interrupting issues for them: the inability of the CPC to actually find common ground on anything other than money, the felt resentment of the grassroots, value dissonance, and Western alienation. Mostly, they see Canada as getting worse, weaker, more vulnerable, and harder to live in. These kinds of important questions aren't even being asked inside the Conservative Party of Canada, let alone having the answers provided.

These are the Convoy Conservatives. They may recede into the fabric of the nation someday, fitting tidily into polling calculations, but they are awake now and want their country back—they want to see the heart of truth, justice, and freedom put back into this nation.

As the convoy happened, and before it became labelled as an 'occupation' coupled with 'economic terror' to justify the invocation of the emergency powers, I saw a multi-racial, multi-faith response from the people across the economic strata in this nation coming out to stand for freedom, peacefully protest, and support democracy in Canada.

This was the profile and the spirit of it before it was reframed by the media. Convoy Conservatives will emerge from different races and faiths.

Whatever your view, this eruption brought a sea-change to Canada that has dislodged us from political adolescence as a nation into adulthood. There is an energy and expectancy awakened that has little tolerance for career politicians and an earnest desire for leaders who are called to contend for this nation and its people as an act of devout service. Cynical political pundits say there is no difference between career politicians and what I am talking about here—the Convoy Conservatives can smell the difference.

The quiet truth is that the Freedom Convoy did accomplish something. The vaccine mandate for the truckers was not enforced, and travel restrictions for citizens were lifted shortly afterwards. Canada has learned from this. The convoy made a difference. There will be other tipping points to come where Canadians who love this country will stand again to shape this discussion and our nation. We know there are some big challenges facing Canada and that this is now a war for the soul of our nation.

The gnawing challenge now is how to deal with the fact that the *Constitution of Canada* and the *Charter of Rights and Freedoms* have been made functionally irrelevant by the Liberal Government, having been undefended in any meaningful way by the Conservative Party of Canada, they have been generally diminished and overlooked by our courts which have applied the "living tree doctrine" penned by Lord Sankey in 1929.[11] This doctrine is now elasticating the interpretation of words in our legislation and Constitution to mean something substantively different than what was ever intended by the authors of the legislation.

This 'inch has become a mile' phenomenon enables a social and structural agenda that has persistently been worked through the Canadian court system by actually bypassing the electorate. Why should fundamental and constitutionally-supreme precepts be reinterpreted by the activism of the Supreme Court in order to work around the electorate?

Section 52 of the *Canadian Constitution* establishes that "the *Constitution of Canada* is the supreme law,"[12] but we have let the court guard it rather than our elected representatives in parliament. Many Convoy Conservatives may not know who Lord Sankey is, but I believe they would not struggle with a policy to reform the judiciary and put the Supreme Court back in the confines of the box they were originally designed to exist within.

This is much more than just Western Canadian Alienation.

This painful awareness across Canada is accentuated by a severely disgruntled Western Canada that is tired of being a colony within a colony. This is not the space for discussions about history, Louis Riel, the District of Assiniboia, or the Buffalo Declaration. It is simply to say that the gnawing challenges referred to above are compounded by the severe dissatisfaction with the feeling of being hamstrung by the overreach of the federal government authority and the curtailment of the *Constitution Act* (Section 92) that sets out the provincial legislative powers.[13] When Canada has stabilized and mitigated the current threats, we will need to undertake serious work on constitutional reform, even re-confederation, which is the reforging of Canada.

This matter is so much more serious than the Laurentians talking about the ruffled feathers of Western Canadians who are 'just' upset about energy policy. That is provocative enough.

The regional disdain for the federal government's energy policy from the 1980s still has burning embers in the Western Canadian psyche, but David Lametti's comments about rescinding the 1930s *Natural Resource Transfer Agreements* that will strip away their constitutional authority will simply pour gasoline on things.

As I write this, the three prairie Premiers have written to Justin Trudeau to have him clarify his position and confirm that David Lametti was not speaking on behalf of the federal government.[14] Can you imagine that a back-room strategist and Justice Minister like David Lametti would ever decide to go rogue and announce the nullification of nearly a hundred-year arrangement on his own?

While I truly value federalism in Canada, I can also observe and understand how many Canadians may rather have a smaller geographical area and a new flag that symbolizes their value framework rather than labouring over the notion of a federal constitutional construct that seems to have fallen out of favour on many fronts.

The broken (and currently unrepaired and unreplaced) statue(s) of the father of confederation, Sir John A. MacDonald, silently screams an awkward question to all Canadians: If it doesn't matter that the statue of the man that is credited with forging Canada by building a national railway is shattered into pieces through a vandalous act, how can it be argued that the values that emanate from this symbol of confederation matter either?

This statue of Sir John A. MacDonald arguably represents the most galvanizing historical event in our history in so much as it is emblematic of the completion of the railway.

In the same way, federalism is the constitutional expression of that event.

Perhaps the deconstructionists that removed the statue just thought that millions of Canadians would not notice if this part of their history was erased. It is entirely possible that those revisionists never actually stopped to think that the removal of the statue of Sir John A. MacDonald might also be interpreted to mean that Western Canadians were legitimately released from the economic and electoral imbalances created by Upper and Lower Canada to subsidize themselves at the expense of the west. This is the big problem with sloppy intellectual deconstructionism—there are unanticipated events like millions of Western Canadians looking at this message and saying something like, "As goes MacDonald, so goes our obligation to federalism."

A fusion of powerful forces now surpasses our historical understanding of Western alienation. The synergy of these forces may actually provide the impetus required to be capable of birthing a new nation that is unreliant upon the old predetermined constitutional pathways established to ensure that it was next to impossible for anyone to get any ideas about the actual partitioning of the nation of Canada.

If the *Charter of Rights and Freedoms* can be disregarded, the *Constitution of Canada* elasticized beyond defensible recognition, and 1930s Treaties rescinded that were protected by Section 92 of the *Constitution Act*, then the provisions within the Constitution that define how Canada may be separated should not be too difficult to circumvent as well. After all, what is good for the goose is good for the gander, right? Self-determination is certainly a more efficient remedy than constitutional reform when Gollum controls the ring and doesn't want to let go.

All of this is compounded by a lurching towards the left that is awakening the normally accommodating sleeping majority of Canadians. This is long past the gay marriage debate. Most Canadians don't have a problem with those in a homosexual relationship receiving the same tax, inheritance, or benefits as a heterosexual couple.

The challenge now is that there is a darker agenda within the LGBTQ movement that wants to weaponize their perspective and insist upon everyone else's validation of their lifestyle choices, the sexualization of our children, and the normalization of pedophilia. These are simply too many steps that are going too far, awakening people to this battleground and the political landscape in which it is being fought. There are Convoy Conservatives who have never been a member of the Conservative Party of Canada, and there are newly activated citizens who may not have previously voted that will aggregate toward and contend against these issues as common rally points.

When all of these forces—the breakdown of institutional safeguards, maturation of the political citizen and protestor, Western separatism, the lurch ideologically left, assault upon parental authority, disdain for the Christian right, the failure of legacy parties to perceive, let alone acknowledge, foreign interference, the integrity of our election process, a lack of serious response to value issues, the selling out of our nation with debt, and a general disdain shown by the mainstream media towards Canadians who do not align with the left—come together, you start to see the profile of a Convoy Conservative forming.

The Convoy Conservatives are not a barbaric hoard. They are sensible, peace-loving, hard-working, tax-paying, family-loving Canadians who are no longer satisfied with the blindness and shallow ideology of the fiscal conservative game theory focussed upon power—they know Canada needs more than a Harper 2.0 redo personified in Poilievre. These citizens are both outside and inside the Conservative Party. They are the non-voters in Canada who are waking up and caring about what is happening to their country and the value system that makes it work.

These people are politically homeless and much bigger than the 5% vote that went to Maxime Bernier in 2021. Some may still *hold their noses* and stay within the Conservative Party of Canada, believing in the priority to remove JT—but time and events may just show the hollowness of Poilievre's house of sand. Poilievre's caustic behaviour, other intervening events, and how fast the former Reform Party members, social conservatives, and the Christian right take to wake up to the CPC's opinion of them and the CPC's woke orientation will all be strong factors now. If you don't know what I am referring to here, please review Chapter Five on learned behaviour.

These citizens have resolve. Many have already been incarcerated on principle, and these Convoy Conservatives have watched what the government has done to non-compliant pastors, with their significant dissatisfaction for these kinds of events being felt by the religious and non-religious alike. Many other people in Canada simply will not be tamed by any government that thinks their freedom is a privilege that can be taken away.

There is a naïve insinuation that Convoy Conservatives don't understand real freedom.

These Convoy Conservative citizens will not be made into cartoon Canadians or political caricatures of brute beasts who have a base instinct to be free but don't understand that freedom comes with responsibility.

This is the cheap trick of every bully class that seeks to control by minimizing the voice of their opponent, then dehumanizing their cognitive function and value compass. The reality for Convoy Conservatives is quite the contrary. They fully understand this and clearly perceive, just as Harper did twenty years ago, that the logical conclusion of what he described as dark moral nihilism will end in "the actual banning of conservative views."[15]

I have already called this dark moral nihilism 'evil' and suggested Harper simply lacked the moral courage to call it that. It will show itself to be as evil as the cold greed of slavery, the institutional destruction of the individual as a social construct within communism, or the genocidal massacre of Romani, homosexuals, and Jews in Nazi Germany.

Is banning the individuals who value and contend for the *Charter of Rights and Freedoms*, protecting religious and family values, even a possibility? Harper clearly seems to think that is within the scope of possibility. As already noted, he says, "The logical end of this thinking is the actual banning of conservative views, which some legislators and 'rights' commissions openly contemplate."[16]

Perhaps you don't see, think, or believe that individuals

with conservative views are already being banned. We are permitting a society to be built where there is very soon to be no freedom of speech, as observed with the passing of Bill C-11;[17] there are emerging segregation laws in public spaces if you happen to be anyone that disagrees with drag queens indoctrinating children, and the rights of some are being subverted for the rights of others through 'non-white only' events exemplified by those introduced in the two Ontario school boards. The banning is happening incrementally. The challenge is that there is a distinct lag in the observation of the banning by the actual victims that are banned.

What will we do if a Christian pastor, or anyone who disagrees with the sexualization of children and drag queens, wants to ride on the same bus travelling anywhere from a public library? Well, we could put the pastor in a 'silent zone' at the back of the bus reserved for Canada's second or third-class citizens. If anything is said to object to this segregation, we could fine them $25,000.00 because anything they say will be subjectively perceived as critical of LGBTQ ideologies, activating the equitable discrimination laws.[18] Ontario Legislative Bill 94 2023 clearly anticipates such a fine for violating prescribed safety zones created for 2SLGBTQ+ people.[19]

As I write this paragraph, on April 8, 2023, Riley Gaines, an American female athlete and swimmer, was punched and beaten at San Francisco State University by a transgender male protestor.[20] Ms. Gaines was speaking at the event on the topic of women's rights and transgender people competing in women's sports. She had to escape the physical assault by fleeing from her podium and locking herself in a room.

This was not just an attack on Ms. Gaines but on the identity of women everywhere—it is an attack on life-giving femininity. Allegedly, the protestors demanded money from the police in order for Ms. Gaines to have safe passage out of the building. Is our society seriously going to stand for the physical beating and ransoming of our mothers, sisters, and daughters? I accept that this was in the United States, but do you think we are much further from this kind of bullying and oppression here in Canada?

Convoy Conservatives are citizen patriots who have properly discerned that by exercising the Canadian value of tolerance exemplified in 'live and let live' or 'do no harm to others,' they have now become the enemy because they disagree with the curtailment of their freedom and the disdain for the things they value. They understand it will only get worse until it is stopped. The choice before them is to either deny who they are and what they believe or to fight for it.

The corrosive problem is the Conservative Party of Canada is not even talking about stopping this unravelling of the nation, it cannot compete with the left-racing left. This party may slow the leftward motion down a bit, but they will always lose this race while they author their own oblivion. This is simply a timing matter. If these forces were not at work and Canada was stable, I would simply just be minded to let the party self-destruct as they steer left.

The existential challenge is that Canada may be irreparably damaged or lost before the Conservative Party of Canada is observed by enough people to have foolishly stretched its tent a mile wide using tent pegs that are only an inch long. The nation is clearly vulnerable and is being led down a path to its own Marxist dystopia, a post-national vassal state of debt servitude, if not economic slavery, of the people of Canada.

Poilievre is piping his tune, promising prosperity without the prescient mind of his predecessor on the matter of values. Harper knew that you could not fight the degradation of a nation's values with economic policy and financial self-interest, in the same way that generations of Canadians know that it is community values personified in good neighbours who might save your life if your vehicle broke down in the middle of Saskatchewan in January.

Our current context makes Harper's 2003 observation even more salient: "In this environment, serious conservative parties simply cannot shy away from values questions."[21] The Convoy Conservatives recognize this truth and will pick their faith, freedom, the health of their family, and secure community over extra cash in their pocket every single time—especially if the extra cash doesn't come with the first four.

It seems this Piper thinks he learned how to tame the social conservatives in 2006, believing they will not 'peep' again now for him. The challenge with this is that no one has seriously considered how the aforementioned forces at work in Canada are causing people to decouple from their cultural, ideological, and religious norms, morals and values and that this will wake them up at some point, turning them into discerning political orphans who look deeper into why Canada is unravelling.

It is starting to appear that the Convoy Conservatives may actually be the true conservatives in Canada, and the CPC is getting in the way by preventing the formation and existence of a real right-wing conservative party that responsibly fuses astute fiscal responsibility with a responsible social policy that provides security, prosperity, community health, and freedom.

Edmund Burke, a British parliament member and one of the philosophical fathers of eighteenth-century conservatism, would have been proud of the seeds of true conservatism germinating within the 'Convoy Conservatives' even in their current unrefined form. Burke wisely challenged the English parliament to approach the American pre-revolution colonists very carefully, perceiving that the colonists possessed a very clear and innate understanding of the legitimacy of government to be dependent upon the cohesive relationship between power and the respect for the values that the colonist's civil liberties were established upon, especially when they were rooted in the inalienable freedoms prescribed by God.[22] This is a potent lesson for all current politicians in Canada in 2023.

Values actually matter. The political order must be disrupted on the right because it has become philosophically anemic and lost sight of this important cohesion. The 'renaissance' is happening already. It is from the bottom up and is still difficult to precisely define.

A young Canadian Muslim's view on the Freedom Convoy.

In the autumn of 2022, I met some friends returning from a road trip. They were all travelling together, one with a large fifth-wheel camper and the other with a 4x4 that was heavily covered with freedom stickers and Canadian flags (none with profanities on them). They parked on the road beside an urban greenspace in Calgary SW, it was a small city park left as an oasis of green amid a large middle-class housing development. One person was an Albertan chicken farmer, the other was an Albertan construction contractor, and the third was a French Canadian who came west with the tide following the convoy's departure from Ottawa. A sidewalk ran along the edge of the road between the parked trucks and the grass that people in the neighbourhood used to walk on, taking them between where we were sitting and the vehicles.

We ended up talking to a lot of people that evening as they curiously walked past, but there was one young man in particular who really surprised me. He was about 25 and had walked past us a couple of times. He told us he had come to Canada with his parents from Syria and that his parents were Muslim. He told my friend that he liked his truck, thanking us for standing up for his rights and those of his friends of the same age. It was fascinating to learn from him that although many people his age supported the principles that they understood the convoy to represent, they didn't like the posture of the government as it reminded them of what their families had left behind in their journey to Canada.

We thanked him for his comments, and out of interest, I asked him if he would support those same principles in another expression of freedom if it happened. He said he might but was scared to, as were his friends. With so much student debt, he told us he could not risk losing

135

his job or being tagged on social media as a protestor for fear of hurting his career. He actually understood the shortsightedness of this in relation to protecting democracy, telling us that we did not really need their help and were doing a good job.

There is a lot within this story to reflect upon.

The Convoy Conservative is also the new immigrant who has felt and directly observed tyranny in their country of origin, wondering what Canada is doing to itself. They are often people with clear religious perspectives who came to Canada for the symbolic image and promises of what we used to be about—democracy, freedoms entrenched by constitutional statutes where you can 'live and let live,' and to be secure and prosper. New Canadians are observing that Canada is stumbling, and they will inevitably find their voices, especially when their religious freedoms are challenged or curtailed.

This is where the real conversation of the rebirth of the conservative right starts. Like a diamond, these many facets of Canadian society discussed in this chapter are forming a movement of people that I believe will shape the political landscape on the right in the next ten years and beyond.

This is the promise Canada has whispered to generations of Canadians, and the magnetism and power to deliver it is still resident within the foundation stones that this nation was built upon.

The power of this message simply needs to be unearthed again.

So, what does this look like? The next chapter discusses

some of the key steps necessary to restore Canada and establish it for a secure, prosperous, free, and healthy future.

9

CHAPTER NINE

There Is Hope. Repairing Walls and Gates. Building Lampstands

Hope starts with awareness. Awareness reveals the choices we need to make.

There is a poignant story about the Jewish people who were carried off into exile by the Persians in the 5th Century BC. The story is told by a slave called Nehemiah, and he makes it clear that the Jews made themselves vulnerable to losing their nation and were ultimately banished into exile because they lived in a way that failed to honour minimum standards established to direct, sustain, and shape their society.[1]

When the Jewish people were conquered, the Persians destroyed their cities, specifically breaking Jerusalem's city walls and gates. Many people were killed, a few escaped, and many of the best were carried off into exile as slaves, where they were to be trained to become Persians. The Persians knew that if they destroyed the walls and the gates of Jerusalem, it would be very difficult for the Jews to reform as a people, let alone form an aspiration to rebuild their nation.

The walls were important in ancient cities because they provided a force-multiplying defence that secured their identity, their people, and their nation. The walls didn't just make it harder to attack—they also contained the gates of their civilization. The gates of the city defined their society because they could determine what and who could enter the city. The gates were the apparatus that opened and closed in order to 'steer' their society, controlling their trade, information systems, education system, social and family infrastructure, religion, and what was allowed to enter to entertain them. The gates were a metaphor for the point of control and function of their government.

One day in exile, a Jewish man named Nehemiah came to the awareness of the desperate condition of the Jewish people and what they had done to cause them to be scattered, confused, and led into slavery. Grieved by this awareness and the condition of his nation, he prayed out to God in his despair, acknowledging what had happened. With this posture, Nehemiah apologized to God for what his people had done to contribute to the chaos and destruction of their society. His acknowledgement of what had happened and his repentant prayer marked a reflection point that enabled a change direction for his nation. Then, this Jewish servant had the audacity to ask the Persian king to release him to rebuild the walls and gates and was given the favour to do so.

The story is famous, and the Jewish slave led the rebuilding of the walls and re-established the gates of Jerusalem, thereby beginning the restoration and independence of Israel. It is a potent story, well known to people of the Jewish and Christian faiths alike. It teaches about God's involvement in the future of His people and their nation—and that He cares about individual lives and how society functions. It also teaches that if a nation chooses to recognize that it has failed to meet these minimum standards for doing life, it may also choose to course-correct, changing direction to restore its security, prosperity, and health.

This story has a direct application to Canada, with our society's walls and gates attacked and damaged, causing the destruction and plundering of what we understand our nation to be, what we desire it to stand for, and how we long for it to function. Much of what I have written in the last eight chapters outlines how this is happening and who lacked the courage and failed to do their job or even recognize the patterns. We can all see and feel the changes in our society and how it is being broken apart, yet somehow, we are afraid to publicly acknowledge that there is a spiritual reality and that we are in a spiritual battle as well as an ideological and political battle.

How is it that even as I write this chapter, I could almost feel impolite for ultimately saying that this is a spiritual battle between good and evil and that evil must not be permitted to unravel Canada? Conservatives in Canada need a new multi-dimensional paradigm to begin to deal with the leftist evil damaging our walls and gates.

Many Canadians have had this very truth hidden from them. The most powerful truths are always ignored, diminished, obfuscated, and maligned by those that have the most to lose from them being vocalized, activated, and applied. It has been too long since this truth has been spoken about as a framework for shaping how we are governed in this nation, as we have forgotten the spiritual in the realm of the temporal.

We should not be surprised, nor should we feel awkward or

We should not be surprised, nor should we feel awkward or impolite about addressing this, especially when our nation is in such deep trouble.

impolite about addressing this, especially when our nation is in such deep trouble. There are truths written into the very centre of our Parliament buildings in Ottawa. These are ancient truths with evident markers left by Canadians for Canadians. In so many ways, this is a covenant between those Canadians and God, for Canada, that continues to this day. I don't care that the revisionists or deconstructionist Marxists don't like these facts. It seems politeness stops us from having too many conversations that we simply must have now.

The apex of intellectual enlightenment is not moral nihilism that inevitably leads to disorder, rebellion, and chaos; it is the humility to identify that you have a mind and a spirit, acknowledging that you will ultimately worship something. God-given freedom allows the choice to determine what you worship. This is the freedom that built our nation.

Our Canadian ancestors left clues for what the right choice is. I respect all Canadians' freedom to choose, but this does not mean the destruction of Canada and the values that it was built on needs to be accommodated while some kind of degenerative 'long game' is played as we race to the bottom and the destruction of our nation. It is time to contend again for the principles that built this nation. This time, it is about returning to an understanding of good and evil and making a choice.

When does an attack on the values that built the nation become an attack on the nation?

We seemed to be ok with the statue of Sir John A. MacDonald being removed as a symbol of the confederation of our nation and its people. In so many ways, Sir John A. MacDonald represented and became the national personification of how federalism was birthed in Canada. Sections 91 and 92 of the *Canadian Constitution* define how our nation shares power between the federal government and the provinces, which is only relevant because there was a nation woven together by a railroad. Have we considered what else is being broken, or removed, along with the brass statues of our first Prime Minister?

Are we going to be comfortable with the Peace Tower also being deconstructed because it elevates the values of truth, justice, freedom, faith, honour, and righteousness? All of these values are directly rooted in dozens of religious texts which are sacred to millions of Canadians and point directly to the God of Abraham, Isaac, and Jacob as the supreme Creator, who is clearly still publicly honoured in Canada within the 'stone, glass, bronze'—as well as human hearts.

Darkness and evil will never be dispelled by fiscal policy; they are dispelled by light. Light emanates from God and the values and truth embedded in our nation's acknowledgment of the supremacy of God.

It is time for Canada to reconnect again to these truths and apply them to our nation's government. We need to re-integrate this wiring back into how this nation operates and our public discourse. When we do this, we will

143

elevate truth, justice, and freedom as values that root and guide government for each and every individual citizen in Canada, supported by a government whose mandate is to serve the Canadian people first. Opportunity, security, and prosperity will thrive for all Canadians in this environment. This is what Canada is about.

Darkness plans to bury the original design and intent for Canada. Numerous examples of this death-by-a-thousand-cuts have been presented across these pages. It is becoming increasingly difficult to argue that there is not a sinister agenda to remake Canada in the image of something very different—the eternal enemy of the values and principles that built the nation we love.

So, what do we need to start to fix this mess in Canada?

As individuals, we can begin by thinking about the simple bedrock issues that define our identity and values, considering how we want to relate to the state and its governmental mechanism that provides the structure we choose to live within.

We need to:

1. Realize that there is good and evil and every Canadian has the innate ability to discern and choose between the two daily;

2. Remember that we have built a nation around peace, truth, justice, prosperity, security, opportunity, loving our neighbour as ourselves, and not doing harm to others;

3. Recognize that we have an ingrained cultural

upbringing (training even) that divides each of us as individuals into two parts. These two parts create discomfort in us when we try to integrate what we think privately into what we say, do, and build publicly. We need to find our integrated voice that can present, influence, and impact the public square without duality;

4. Re-activate and apply the understanding of truth and light back into our school boards, municipalities, provinces, and federal government;

5. Create the space for gathering groups of people that carry and champion this light of freedom, joining them together to build permanent lampstands in the nation so that Canada is repaired, restored, and strengthened;

6. Acknowledge and apologize for forgetting about these truths and allowing the lampstand in the public square to be taken down, then find ways to help the nation change course;

7. Empower and demand the truth. Repeat;

8. Catalyze a counter-response to darkness and create the deep change needed to repair the walls and gates of our nation.

Then together, we can reform the direction of this nation and build solid governmental policy for all Canadians that:

Enshrines the inherent value of each and every individual.

Guarantees freedom of thought, conscience, belief, and

religion, shrinks government, empowers our citizens, ensures freedom of the press, and secures and defends our borders and our people.

Recognizes the family as the primary building block rooted in the primacy of parental authority, re-establishing priorities in education that will innovate, create, build, and strengthen Canada.

Empowers our citizens, unleashes opportunity and resources for all Canadians, strengthens communities, incentivizes and repatriates industry and entrepreneurship, enables mechanisms that support generational wealth, and establishes this nation securely for the generations that follow.

Reforges our nation as one people, with one blood, operating in one law, and establishes the people of Canada as the legitimate sovereign in this nation in order to complete our confederation.

Places the past in the past with true reconciliation and builds a nation from the strength of the lessons learned.

This is the kind of Canada that I believe we can build if we engage and contend for the value framework that built this nation again.

Money and prosperity with security follow solid values; this is how we can build a strong and secure nation for all Canadians. Just like with the story of Nehemiah, change starts with each and every Canadian deciding to individually respond, change direction and find new communities to align around a purpose that will complete and secure the reforging of this nation. This process starts with engaging in real conversations about what is actually happening in our country— it begins with the truth.

Saint Augustine of Hippo, the famous 5th-century philosopher, is known for saying, "Truth is like a lion; you don't have to defend it. Let it loose; it will defend itself."

Host no fear.

Vincit veritas—the truth wins.

APPENDIX A

Article—*The Great Reset: Deconstruction of Canadian Sovereignty*

The Great Reset: Deconstruction of Canadian Sovereignty
Grant Abraham
22 November 2020

Covid-19 is a Trojan Horse for a national Re-set that is both suspiciously unclear and chillingly sinister in its portent. This article connects some of the dots between the innocuous coded syntax of the UN 2030 Agenda for Sustainable Development to the working brief from one of the six working groups (name intentionally withheld) detailing how Canada will be prepared for this change and what life will look like after the re-set.

It is with profound regret that I must write this article as an alarm for our nation, for the plans that are underway in this re-set have the clear purpose to unravel our way of life, re-define our understanding of prosperity and rob us of the hope, aspirations and promise that have made this nation great for so many generations. We must act now if we are going to provide the same hope and opportunity for our children and grandchildren.

With gratefulness, I acknowledge the proactivity of my friend, who shall remain anonymous at this time, for having taken the risk to provide me with a copy of the working brief and notes from one of the committees established and funded by our Liberal Government. The primary goals of this working brief are to: a) redefine the fundamental values of a democratic society, b) expand the government's role in the private life of citizens under the auspices of climate change, c) establish a new definition of prosperity, and d) redefine economic, education and governance models. All of this is done in the shadows without scrutiny from parliament.

The context for this working committee is defined in Section 45 of the UN 2030 Agenda. Representatives from the Federal, Provincial, Municipal and Aboriginal governments, as well as other actors from civil society, sit on this committee.

The working notes start with a call for a New Approach to Sustainability, "because our blind spots are so deeply ingrained in our thinking that we just accept them as fact." Therefore, the working brief's 'Theory of Change' is predictable. It says: "Reality is just a construct that requires a fundamentally new approach." The premise is that our framework of thought and the societal systems that exist to support our frameworks of thought simply need to be re-thought, de-constructed and re-built because our current values and worldview are deemed to be "incorrect" according to this committee. What is an incorrect value? Who judges this? What specific new values will replace the old?

This committee's work is to do this job so that our economic, governance, and education systems are ready for a harmonized alignment with whatever is imagined as the alternative system of governance for

Canada. The working notes set out key tasks, a few of which will be commented on below.

Let's start with "Re-defining Prosperity." The preamble acknowledges that, "For many people, the notion of prosperity is closely associated with the increase of material wealth." I might add here that the implication is that this is the increase of material wealth that one "owns" which of course refers to our current understanding of holding wealth.

The un-named writers of this document want to deconstruct this value. They say, "We need a new concept of prosperity." We need a new one because, "the wealthy use energy and materials, creating more waste and greater carbon emissions." These un-named writers re-imagine "prosperity" as "meet[ing] our human needs and aspirations while staying within ecological limits."

A red flag is how the committee demonizes our framework for prosperity and how they reframe it to resemble something very different.

Please note also that this re-definition of the word "prosperity" in the working brief has direct correlative roots with Section 27 of the UN 2030 Social Development Goals that states, "...inclusive and sustainable economic growth is essential for prosperity. This will only be possible if wealth is shared and income inequality is addressed." As a result, the new concept of prosperity will re-distribute wealth to ensure fewer inequalities between citizens.

The notes go on to say that the following areas of action are aimed at re-defining and re-imagining prosperity.

The plan promotes policies that allow us to "individually and collectively, meet our basic needs, to create meaning in our lives and enjoy a good quality of life with low environmental impacts." This is very different from building wealth for our families and the generations that follow us. In this new plan, goods, services and available resources are equitably dispensed to all—there is even a prosperity index to "track" our well-being including rewards and punishments. Please carefully note the movement from our current understanding, where we increase personal wealth that we own, to a system where our needs are simply met and dispensed to us collectively.

The re-definition of the word prosperity is the most insidious element in this working brief. It inherently requires the re-allocation of property. This means that property is not owned by the individual but by the government to be enjoyed collectively. How could that ever happen you ask? Well, read on.

"Re-defining our Systems" includes a redesign of our economic systems, governance, education and infrastructure," (and a working committee is already established for each) because "the current structure of our governance makes it difficult to implement significant change with rewards and punishment for unsustainable behavior."

Eight-hundred years of entrenched rights, liberties and property that are now enshrined in our rule of law are surely inconvenient for those who wish to restructure our governance model, re-distribute property and re-allocate wealth to make sure there are no disparities.

Another redefinition of society mentioned in the brief is the migration to a universal wage for subsistence for all in classic Marxist style. While this working group is aware that this policy re-design will have "major impacts on certain sectors of society," they assuage themselves with the acknowledgement that if they adopt "a leadership position on sustainability, the benefits will far outweigh the drawbacks."

When I asked my intrepid friend what they understood all these oblique objectives meant after having sat in hours of discussion on the matter, they told me that it would "alter our government structure with total government breakdown...that it is the deconstruction of our systems from within." This is not a dystopian daydream unless the Liberal Government now funds daydreams to the tune of Six Million Dollars per year (and that is just for this one committee). I believe this raises profound questions about the legitimacy of this minority Liberal Government and those that support its mandate in our House of Parliament.

Thomas Hobbes, a famous English Legal Theorist, observed that the legitimacy of a government does not emanate from a successful election result; rather, the government's ability to protect its citizens sustains its legitimacy to govern. The logic follows that if a government cannot, or will not, protect its citizens, it is therefore no longer legitimate.

The thorny issue revolves around this concept of "protection" and the important job of assessing what actions are necessary, proportionate and reasonable to protect us. Covid-19 certainly creates an environment where citizens will be quick to appreciate protection. Not surprisingly, Mr. Trudeau has noted that "the pandemic has provided an opportunity for a re-set," and I wonder whether this wonderful sounding "re-imagining" to protect us from our allegedly wasteful and inequitable society might be a Trojan Horse that carries something much worse.

Is this how the German people felt in 1935 when they woke up and realized that Hitler's intoxicating words meant something very different? Mr. Trudeau needs to be cautioned that if his agenda in this "re-set" is to restructure the underpinnings our society, its laws and rights of property in these ways, he must understand that he has not been given this mandate by the people, and this nefarious policy agenda is outside the mandate (ultra vires) of this government's authority. As a minimum, it requires constitutional reform, and this must be preceded by an election that outlines the reset agenda in a clear manifesto.

If he persists in bankrupting our nation and undermining the systems that support our way of life for the principle of sustainable development, he may choose to review Section 46 of the Criminal Code that sets out the conditions for treason. There is a reason why our founders ensured the Minister of Justice be appointed by the Governor General and why our honourable Armed Forces and the Royal Canadian

Mounted Police swear allegiance to Her Majesty the Queen, not the Prime Minister. The stakes are very high. Public sentiment requires that Mr. Trudeau and his handlers think carefully on this caution.

I am not ready to see our sovereignty forfeited. I believe the rest of our patriotic citizens who value the dignity of work along with peace, order and good government will feel the same way once they understand what is at stake. God keep our land glorious and free.

Grant Abraham

APPENDIX B

Email Correspondence with Pierre Poilievre

[Subject:]Multi-tiered intergovernmental shadow committee to support Reset

Wed, Dec 9, 2020, 12:47 PM

to pierre. poilievre

The Right Honourable Pierre Poilievre MP,

You do not know me but I am a Lawyer and a member of the Conservative Party of Canada. I write today to provide you with important information on the reset which I note you have recently attempted to illuminate for Canadians. This research supports your theory that there is an assault on Canada's rights and freedoms. I believe this may be the most profound threat our young nation has ever faced.

This article's title may seem somewhat cliche now, it reveals the work of a not-for-profit organization in BC that is funded by the Liberal Government (6 million Annually) and is actively working as a multi-tiered intergovernmental agency to re-wire Canadian values, develop new policies to reflect re-defined values that are seeking to deconstruct Canadian governance in order to align with a globalist UN 2030 Agenda.

It is my view that when all of the anomalies in our political discourse and dilution of charter right/civil liberties are aggregated, they reveal a policy trajectory that would never be accepted if their aggregate was held in the light of parliament, or a motion was brought to amend our constitution to effect these changes.

This group is working without the scrutiny of parliament but with directives that appear to be directly from the PM. The source of my information is an elected municipal official that sits on this committee. The extracts in the article are taken from working notes used in the evolution of the committee's thought which I possess. I have not identified names here but will share the sources with trusted officials if requested by you.

Thank you for reviewing this. I sincerely hope it may contribute to informing thought and framing a response for people who are deeply concerned about the erosion of our culture and values in Canada.

Grant Abraham

Poilievre, Pierre - M.P.   Jan 29, 2021,
<pierre.poilievre@parl.gc.ca>   8:55 PM

Thank you for sharing your thoughts with me, Grant.

Trudeau has from the start viewed COVID as an opportunity for a power grab. He even tried to give himself the power to raise any tax to any level at any time over the next two years. I successfully led the effort to stop him.

Here are the facts:

Justin Trudeau told a United Nations conference that "this pandemic has provided an opportunity for a reset. This is our chance to accelerate our pre-pandemic efforts to reimagine economic systems...".

Please be assured that I will keep fighting to defend our rights and freedoms. We need the government to focus instead on protecting the lives and livelihoods of hardworking people.

Sincerely,
Pierre Poilievre P.C., M.P. Carleton
Shadow Minister of Finance
JL

ENDNOTES

Epigraph
1. (Bloedow, 2020, p. 84) Note: page numbers for the Kindle edition may vary based on the size of the viewing window used to access this resource.
2. Text as copied from the image of the window itself (Bloedow, 2020, p. 84).

Chapter 1
1. Another version of this text is commonly attributed to Edmund Burke: "The only thing necessary for the triumph of evil is for good men to do nothing."

Chapter 2
1. (Canada Strong and Free Network, 2023, 0:35–2:20)
2. (Canada Strong and Free Network, 2023)
3. (Angus Reid Institute, 2023)
4. (Kheiriddin, 2022)
5. (Kheiriddin, 2022, Chapter 4)
6. (Kheiriddin, 2022, Chapter 5)

Chapter 3
1. This chapter comprises an expanded version of my article, originally published in the Western Standard on March 5, 2022, titled: *Canadians are being bullied into a new social contract* (Abraham, 2022a).
2. (The Constitution Acts, 1867 to 1982, 1867, sec. 91) See also (Centre for Constitutional Studies, 2019b)
3. (National Security and Intelligence Committee of Parliamentarians, 2020, p. 77, para. 189)
4. (cpac, 2020, 13:44–14:10)
5. (cpac, 2020, 29:21–29:43)
6. (CBC, 2010)
7. (Global News, 2020, 2:06)
8. (Schwab & Malleret, 2020)
9. (*Canadian Charter*, 1982, s 6(2)(b))
10. (McKay, 2023)
11. (Lawson, 2015)
12. (Abraham, 2022b)

13. (Global News, 2020, 2:06)
14. (Government of Canada, 2023)
15. (United Nations, 2015)
16. (Darrell Vermilion, 2020, 0:07)
17. (United Nations, 1992)
18. (Confidential, personal communication, n.d.) Please note that the identity of the individual and key identifying characteristics are intentionally left anonymous.
19. (Confidential, personal communication, n.d.)
20. (Confidential, personal communication, n.d.)
21. (United Nations, 2007), (Department of Justice Canada, 2020)

Chapter 4
1. (Wells, 2013, pp. 58–59)
2. (Statistics Canada, 2021, p. 1)
3. (*Bill 15, an Act to amend the Youth Protection Act and other legislative provisions*, 2022)
4. (*Legislative Summary of Bill C-6: An Act to amend the Criminal Code (conversion therapy)*, 2020), (*Legislative Summary of Bill C-4: An Act to amend the Criminal Code (conversion therapy)*, 2021)
5. (*Legislative Summary of Bill C-6: An Act to amend the Criminal Code (conversion therapy)*, "2.2 New Offences (Clause 5)")
6. (Boisvert, 2021)
7. (Hon. E. Fast, personal communication, May 25, 2023)
8. (Canada, Parliament, 2023, pp. 54–65) See the section titled "Mature Minors"–"Recommendation 19" and "Recommendation 16" in particular.
9. (Parliament of Canada, n.d.) Note that Michael Cooper is one of the vice-chairs of this committee.
10. (Wells, 2013, pp. 58–59)

Chapter 5
1. (Steacy, 2023)
2. (cpac, 2022a)
3. (Wells, 2006, p. 314)
4. (Wells, 2006, p. 314)
5. (The Canadian Press & Ritchie, 2023), (McGregor, 2023)
6. (Bannon's War Room—Bio and Archives, 2022)
7. (Rebel News Canada, 2023, 2:38–3:03, 5:35–5:51)
8. (cpac, 2022b, 3:39:44)

9. ("Definition of Righteous," 2023)
10. (Levant, 2023)
11. (Levant, 2023)
12. (National Council, 2020, sec. 3c)
13. (cpac, 2020, 13:35–13:44)
14. (cpac, 2020, 13:44–14:33)
15. (cpac, 2020, 25:50–26:10)
16. (cpac, 2020, 29:15–30:35)
17. (cpac, 2020, 13:44–14:33)
18. (cpac, 2020, 13:44–14:33)
19. (Cooper, 2023a), (Cooper, 2023b)
20. Leslyn Lewis posted on Twitter about foreign interference starting February, 2023 (Lewis, n.d.). On March 1, 2023, she retweeted two short clips, including one of Pierre Poilievre (Lewis, 2023a), (Lewis, 2023b).
21. (P. Poilievre, personal communication, March 1, 2023a) Note: As of the date of this publication, this tweet appears to be no longer publicly visible and is therefore cited as personal communication.
22. Despite retweeting a French-language clip of his statement published by cpac (cpac, 2023), (P. Poilievre, personal communication, March 1, 2023b), Poilievre did not widely address foreign interference himself using this platform on this date (Poilievre, n.d.).
23. (Confidential, personal communication, n.d.) Note: the identity of this individual and the working papers themselves purposefully remain confidential. References and citations will be listed as personal communication.
24. (United Nations, 2015)
25. (Confidential, personal communication, n.d.) See note 23.
26. (Klokkenluiders, 2023, 2:50)
27. (Klokkenluiders, 2023, 2:50)
28. (Grant & Ward, 2022)
29. (Grant, 2023)
30. (Practo, 2015) Note the difference in wording between the Classic Hippocratic Oath and the Revised Hippocratic oath, which "is widely accepted in today's medical schools."
31. (P. Poilievre, personal communication, Jan 29, 2021) See Appendix B.
32. (P. Poilievre, personal communication, Jan 29, 2021) See Appendix B.

33. (Confidential, personal communication, n.d.), (Global News, 2020, 2:06)

Chapter 6

1. (*Canadian Charter*, 1982, s 6(2)(b))
2. (*The Holy Bible, New International Version NIV,* 2011, Prov. 29:18)
3. (Bloedow, 2020, pp. 30, 101) Note that the translation of this proverb as displayed on the window is taken from the King James Version.
4. The supremacy of God and the rule of law are both concepts inherent in the Magna Carta (The British Library, 2014), which "set the groundwork for our democracy, justice and human rights" (Government of Canada, 2015).
5. (Abraham, 2022b)
6. (*The Holy Bible, New International Version NIV,* 2011, Rev. 22:2)
7. (Ivison, 2023)
8. (Bloedow, 2020)
9. (Allan Smith, 2022, 52:30–53:05) This specific episode of the Catholic Hour is titled "How to Meet Communism" (OTRCAT Inc., n.d., sample episode).
10. (ADF UK, 2023)
11. (The City of Calgary, 2023)
12. (Lewis, 2011)
13. (Lewis, 2011)
14. (Lewis, 2011)
15. (Government of Canada, 2022)

Chapter 7

1. This statement comes from the section heading that introduces the passage of Scripture found in James 2:14–26 NKJV (The Holy Bible, New King James Version, 1982, Jas. 2:14–26).
2. (*The Holy Bible, New International Version NIV,* 2011, Matt. 10:7–8)
3. (*The Holy Bible, New International Version NIV,* 2011, Matt. 28:19–20)
4. (*The Holy Bible, New International Version NIV,* 2011, 2 Cor. 3:17)
5. (Canada Revenue Agency, 2018) The T3010 Registered Charity Information Return is necessary for charities to file in a timely manner lest they risk losing their charitable status (Canada Revenue Agency, 2018).
6. (Canada Revenue Agency, 2012, sec. 1), (Canada Revenue Agency, 2019)
7. (Canada Revenue Agency, 2023) In addition to allocating the

Canada Emergency Response Benefit (CERB) to individuals, the government supported employers, including charities, by providing the Canada Emergency Wage Subsidy (CEWS) and the Canada Emergency Rent Subsidy (CERS) (Canada Revenue Agency, 2023).
8. (Canada Revenue Agency, 2022). Use this online search to view financial statements from the last five years for all registered charities in Canada.
9. (The Holy Bible, New King James Version, 1982, Matt. 10:8)
10. (Allan Smith, 2022, 52:30–53:05)
11. (Pew Research Center, 2013), (Statistics Canada, 2021)
12. (*The Holy Bible, New International Version NIV,* 2011, Matt. 5:13–16, Matt. 13:33)
13. (Debt.ca, 2023), (Hopper, 2022)
14. (Anonymous, personal communication, March 24, 2023)
15. A variation of a quotation commonly attributed to Albert Einstein.
16. (*The Holy Bible, New International Version NIV,* 2011, Rom. 12:4–5)

Chapter 8
1. (Tolkien, 1991)
2. (Claypool, 2022)
3. (K. Bexte, personal communication, Jan 30, 2022) Note: due to the nature of Twitter having only a limited archive space, this video appears to be no longer available for replay.
4. (Anonymous, personal communication, March 24, 2023)
5. (Wells, 2013, pp. 58–59)
6. (Jeremy McKenzie, personal communication, Feb 12, 2022)
7. (Pardy, 2023)
8. (Bradley, 2023)
9. (Bradley, 2023)
10. (Bradley, 2023)
11. (Centre for Constitutional Studies, 2019a)
12. (Amendment to the Constitution Act, 1867, The Constitution Acts, 1867 to 1982, 1982, sec. 52)
13. (The Constitution Acts, 1867 to 1982, 1867, sec. 92)
14. (Harding, 2023)
15. (Wells, 2013, p. 59)
16. (Wells, 2013, p. 58–59)
17. (Raycraft, 2023), (*Bill C-11, An Act to amend the Broadcasting Act and to make related and consequential amendments to other Acts,* 2023)

18. (*Bill 94: An Act to enact the 2SLGBTQI+ Community Safe Zones Act, 2023 and to establish the Ontario 2SLGBTQI+ Safety Advisory Committee*, 2023, sec. 2)
19. (*Bill 94: An Act to enact the 2SLGBTQI+ Community Safe Zones Act, 2023 and to establish the Ontario 2SLGBTQI+ Safety Advisory Committee*, 2023, sec. 4)
20. (Gupta, 2023)
21. (Wells, 2013, p. 59)
22. (Newsom, 2002)

Chapter 9
1. (*The Holy Bible, New International Version NIV,* 2011, Neh.) Please note that subsequent references to the story of Nehemiah refer back to the account contained in this book of the Bible.

REFERENCES

Abraham, G. (2022a, March 5). *ABRAHAM: Canadians are being bullied into a new social contract.* Western Standard. Retrieved June 12, 2023, from https://www.westernstandard.news/opinion/abraham-canadians-are-being-bullied-into-a-new-social-contract/article_9e9db65c-c858-5949-b318-83ca06b58ba5.html

Abraham, G. (2022b, March 18). What Canada Can Learn From Britain's Escape From the European Union. *The Epoch Times.* Retrieved June 16, 2023, from https://www.theepochtimes.com/what-canada-can-learn-from-britains-escape-from-the-european-union_4339667.html

ADF UK. (2023, March 7). BREAKING: Parliament introduces first "thought-crime" into UK law. ADF UK. Retrieved June 19, 2023, from https://adf.uk/parliament-introduces-thought-crime/

Allan Smith. (2022, November 2). *Communism and the Conscience of the West. Archbishop Fulton J. Sheen Catholic Hour Recordings (1947)* [Video]. YouTube. Retrieved June 19, 2023, from https://www.youtube.com/watch?v=TTNyUXfco1A

Amendment to the Constitution Act, 1867, The Constitution Acts, 1867 to 1982. (1982). Part VII, 52 (1). Retrieved from the Justice Laws website on June 19, 2023: https://laws-lois.justice.gc.ca/eng/const/page-13.html#h-59

Angus Reid Institute. (2023). Federal Politics: Liberals trail CPC by six points in vote intention; but Poilievre lags Trudeau in likeability. In Angus Reid Institute. Retrieved June 15, 2023, from https://angusreid.org/federal-politics-trudeau-poilievre-cpc-liberals/

Bannon's War Room—Bio and Archives. (2022, July 12). *Christine Anderson: Serious Vaccine Adverse Events Endangering Passengers Across Europe* [Video]. Canada Free Press. Retrieved June 17, 2023, from https://canadafreepress.com/article/christine-anderson-serious-vaccine-adverse-events-endangering-passengers-across-europe

Bill 15, An Act to amend the Youth Protection Act and other legislative provisions. (2022). 1st Reading Dec. 1, 2022, 42nd

Legislature, 2nd session. Retrieved from the National Assembly of Québec website on June 16, 2023: https://assnat.qc.ca/en/travaux-parlementaires/projets-loi/projet-loi-15-42-2.html

Bill 94: An Act to enact the 2SLGBTQI+ Community Safe Zones Act, 2023 and to establish the Ontario 2SLGBTQI+ Safety Advisory Committee. (2023). 1st Reading Apr. 4, 2023, 43rd Legislature, 1st Session. Retrieved from the Legislative Assembly of Ontario website on June 20, 2023: https://www.ola.org/en/legislative-business/bills/parliament-43/session-1/bill-94 and https://www.ola.org/sites/default/files/node-files/bill/document/pdf/2023/2023-04/b094_e.pdf

Bill C-11, An Act to amend the Broadcasting Act and to make related and consequential amendments to other Acts. (2023). 1st Reading Feb 2, 2022, 44th Parliament, 1st session. Retrieved from the Parliament of Canada website on June 29, 2023: https://www.parl.ca/DocumentViewer/en/44-1/bill/C-11/royal-assent

Bloedow, L. (2020). *The Legacy of 25 Scripture Verses on Parliament Hill: Canadian History With New Eyes* (T. Bloedow, Ed.; Kindle). Christian Roots Canada.

Boisvert, N. (2021, December 1). MPs embrace after bill to ban conversion therapy passes unanimously in House. CBC. Retrieved June 17, 2023, from https://www.cbc.ca/news/politics/conversion-therapyconservatives-1.6269147

Bradley, J. (2023, April 24). Hamilton school board holding racially-segregated employee gathering. *Western Standard.* Retrieved June 19, 2023, from https://www.westernstandard.news/news/hamilton-school-board-holding-racially-segregated-employee-gathering/article_73d4c0cc-e2e9-11ed-b10d-87c8b76470d5.html

Canada, Parliament. Special Joint Committee on Medical Assistance in Dying. (2023). *MEDICAL ASSISTANCE IN DYING IN CANADA: CHOICES FOR CANADIANS.* 44th Parl., 1st sess. Rept. of the Special Joint Committee on Medical Assistance in Dying. Retrieved from the Parliament of Canada website on June 17, 2023: https://parl.ca/DocumentViewer/en/44-1/AMAD/

report-2/page-39#1

Canada Revenue Agency. (2012, October 31). *General requirements for charitable registration*. Government of Canada. Retrieved June 19, 2023, from https://www.canada.ca/en/revenue-agency/services/charities-giving/charities/policies-guidance/guidance-017-general-requirements-charitable-registration.html

Canada Revenue Agency. (2018, October 24). *T3010 charity return –Overview*. Government of Canada. Retrieved June 19, 2023, from https://www.canada.ca/en/revenue-agency/services/charities-giving/charities/operating-a-registered-charity/t3010-charity-return-overview.html

Canada Revenue Agency. (2019, January 24). *Basic guidelines*. Government of Canada. Retrieved June 19, 2023, from https://www.canada.ca/en/revenue-agency/services/charities-giving/charities/checklists-charities/basic-guidelines.html

Canada Revenue Agency. (2022, May 25). *List of charities and certain other qualified donees - basic search*. Government of Canada. Retrieved June 19, 2023, from https://apps.cra-arc.gc.ca/ebci/hacc/srch/pub/dsplyBscSrch?request_locale

Canada Revenue Agency. (2023, January 24). *Report on the Charities Program 2020 to 2021*. Government of Canada. Retrieved June 19, 2023, from https://www.canada.ca/en/revenue-agency/services/charities-giving/charities/about-charities-directorate/report-on-charities-program/report-on-charities-program-2020-2021.html

Canada Strong and Free Network. (2023, April 9). *The Right Honourable Stephen J. Harper keynote speech CSFN 2023*[Video]. YouTube. Retrieved June 13, 2023, from https://www.youtube.com/watch?v=r8csqCV4FV8

Canadian Charter of Rights and Freedoms, s 7, Part I of the Constitution Act, 1982, being Schedule B to the Canada Act 1982 (UK), 1982, c11

CBC. (2010). *Web Exclusive: Full Interview with Richard Fadden* [Video]. CBC. Retrieved June 16, 2023, from https://www.cbc.ca/player/play/1527828910

Centre for Constitutional Studies. (2019a, July 4). *Living Tree Doctrine*. Retrieved June 19, 2023, from:

169

https://www.constitutionalstudies.ca/2019/07/living-tree-doctrine/

Centre for Constitutional Studies. (2019b, July 4). *Peace, Order and Good Government.* Retrieved June 16, 2023, from https://www.constitutionalstudies.ca/2019/07/peace-order-and-good-government/

Claypool, W. (2022, January). *Watch: Convoy Organizers Hold Press Conference With Only Independent Media.* The National Telegraph. Retrieved June 19, 2023, from https://thenationaltelegraph.com/interviews/watch-convoy-organizers-hold-press-conference-with-only-independent-media

Cooper, S. (2023a, February 24). *Liberals ignored CSIS warning on 2019 candidate accused in Chinese interference probe: sources.* Global News. Retrieved June 17, 2023, from https://globalnews.ca/news/9504291/liberals-csis-warning-2019-election-candidate-chinese-interference/

Cooper, S. (2023b, March 22). *Liberal MP Han Dong secretly advised Chinese diplomat in 2021 to delay freeing Two Michaels: sources.* Global News. Retrieved June 17, 2023, from https://globalnews.ca/news/9570437/liberal-mp-han-dong-secretly-advised-chinese-diplomat-in-2021-to-delay-freeing-two-michaels-sources/

cpac. (2020, March 12). *Intelligence review committee releases reports for 2019* [Video]. YouTube. Retrieved June 16, 2023, from https://www.youtube.com/watch?v=OOUkq791x7s

cpac. (2022a, May 11). *Conservative leadership candidates' English-language debate – May 11, 2022* [Video]. YouTube. Retrieved June 17, 2023, from https://www.youtube.com/watch?v=WzDZslpSZ_8

cpac. (2022b, September 10). *Pierre Poilievre wins Conservative leadership –September 10, 2022* [Video]. YouTube. Retrieved June 17, 2023, from https://www.youtube.comwatch?v=UgYzT1xh2Ko

cpac. (2023, March 1). Conservative Leader Urges Inquiry on Foreign Election Interference. Cpac. Retrieved June 17, 2023, from https://www.cpac.ca/episode?id=e083aa6a-3f40-4f55-ada7-a34329716055

Darrell Vermilion. (2020, November 14). *World Economic Forum: The*

Great Reset — You'll own nothing, and you'll be happy [Video].
YouTube. Retrieved June 16, 2023, from https://www.
youtube.com/watch?v=4zUjsEaKbkM

Debt.ca. (2023). *Canada Debt Clock.* Retrieved June 19, 2023, from
https://www.debt.ca/debt-clock

Definition of righteous. (2023). In *Merriam-Webster Dictionary.*
Retrieved June 17, 2023, from https://www.merriam-
webster.com/dictionary/righteous

Department of Justice Canada. (2020, December 3). Government
of Canada introduces legislation respecting the United
Nations Declaration on the Rights of Indigenous Peoples.
Government of Canada. Retrieved June 16, 2023, from
https://www.canada.ca/en/department-justice/
news/2020/12/government-of-canada-introduces-
legislation-respecting-the-united-nations-declaration-on-
the-rights-of-indigenous-peoples.html
Date modified: 2021-01-27.

Global News. (2020, September 29). *Coronavirus: Trudeau tells
UN conference that pandemic provided "opportunity for a reset"*
[Video]. YouTube. Retrieved June 16, 2023, from
https://www.youtube.com/watch?v=n2fp0Jeyjvw

Government of Canada. (2015, February 17). The Magna Carta
in Canada for its 800th Anniversary. *Government of Canada.*
https://www.canada.ca/en/news/archive/2015/02/
magna-carta-canada-800th-anniversary.html

Government of Canada. (2022, October 26). *The Canadian census:
A rich portrait of the country's religious and ethnocultural diversity.*
Statistics Canada — the Daily. Retrieved June 19, 2023,
from https://www150.statcan.gc.ca/n1/daily-
quotidien/221026/dq221026b-eng.htm

Government of Canada. (2023, June 20). *Canada's role in the
development of an international pandemic instrument.* Retrieved
June 16, 2023, from https://www.canada.ca/en/public-
health/services/emergency-preparedness-response/
canada-role-international-pandemic-instrument.html

Grant, M. (2023, January 9). Coutts protest leaders to go on trial
in 2024. *CBC.* Retrieved June 17, 2023, from https://
www.cbc.ca/news/canada/calgary/coutts-protest-border-
blockade-leadership-group-trial-dates-1.6707884

Grant, M., & Ward, R. (2022, November 3). Hundreds show up at Lethbridge courthouse to support men charged in Coutts border blockade. CBC. Retrieved June 18, 2023, from https://www.cbc.ca/news/canada/calgary/convoy-headed-to-lethbridge-courthouse-to-support-freedom-convoy-charged-1.6640337

Gupta, R. (2023, April 7). Terrified swimming champion Riley Gaines is ambushed by screaming trans activists and "hit twice by guy in a dress" after Saving Women's Sports speech at San Fran State University - as cops say there were NO arrests. *Daily Mail*. Retrieved June 20, 2023, from https://www.dailymail.co.uk/news/article-11949057/Terrified-Riley-Gaines-ambushed-screaming-trans-activists-physically-attacked-her.html?dg

Harding, L. (2023, April 12). How a Federal Minister's Remarks Raised Jurisdiction Infringement Fears in the Prairies. *The Epoch Times*. Retrieved June 19, 2023, from https://www.theepochtimes.com/how-a-federal-ministers-remarks-raised-jurisdiction-infringement-fears-in-the-prairies_5185664.html

Hopper, T. (2022, October 31). It's official: Canada ran a $90.2 billion deficit last year. *National Post*. Retrieved June 19, 2023, from https://nationalpost.com/news/canada/its-official-canada-ran-a-90-2-billion-deficit-last-year

Ivison, J. (2023, May 2). John Ivison: Federal government strips religious symbols from crown adorning Royal Coat of Arms. *National Post*. Retrieved June 19, 2023, from https://nationalpost.com/opinion/canada-strips-religious-symbols-from-crown-on-coat-of-arms

Kheiriddin, T. (2022). *The Right Path: How Conservatives Can Unite, Inspire, and Take Canada Forward.* [eBook]. Optimum Publishing International.

Klokkenluiders. [klokkenluiders]. (2023, April 8). *Grappenmakers Vovan en Lexus die zich voordeden als Zelensky bedrogen Christine Lagarde, de President van de Europese Centrale Bank om* [Video attached] [Telegram channel post]. Telegram. https://t.me/klokkenluiders

Lawson, G. (2015, December 8). Trudeau's Canada, Again. The New York Times. Retrieved June 16, 2023, from https://

www.nytimes.com/2015/12/13/magazine/trudeaus-canada-again.html

Legislative Summary of Bill C-4: An Act to amend the Criminal Code (conversion therapy). (2021). 1st Reading Nov. 29, 2021, 44th Parliament, 1st session. Retrieved from the Parliament of Canada website on June 17, 2023: https://lop.parl.ca/sites/PublicWebsite/default/en_CA/ResearchPublications/LegislativeSummaries/441C4E

Legislative Summary of Bill C-6: An Act to amend the Criminal Code (conversion therapy). (2020). 1st Reading Oct. 1, 2020, 43rd Parliament, 2nd session. Retrieved from the Parliament of Canada website on June 16, 2023: https://lop.parl.ca/sites/PublicWebsite/default/en_CA/ResearchPublications/LegislativeSummaries/432C6E

Levant, E. (2023, March 28). *There's a war on Christians in Canada—help us make a documentary about it.* Rebel News. Retrieved June 17, 2023, from https://www.rebelnews.com/theres_a_war_on_christians_in_canada_help_us_make_a_documentary_about_it

Lewis, C. (2011, October 21). Experts weigh in role of Canada's proposed religious freedom office. *National Post.* Retrieved June 19, 2023, from https://nationalpost.com/holy-post/experts-question-the-role-of-canadas-proposed-religious-office

Lewis, L. [@LeslynLewis]. (n.d.). *Tweets & Retweets* [Twitter profile]. Twitter. Retrieved June 17, 2023, from https://twitter.com/LeslynLewis

Lewis, L. [@LeslynLewis]. (2023a, March 1). *It's time for Justin Trudeau to come clean and be transparent with Canadians. Conservatives will not allow Trudeau and his* [Video attached] [Retweet]. Twitter. https://twitter.com/BlaineFCalkins/status/1631069609607458820?cxt=HHwWiMCzyeHK3KItAAAA

Lewis, L. [@LeslynLewis]. (2023b, March 1). *"Justin Trudeau has done nothing but try to intimidate members of CSIS, tried to attack the courageous whistleblowers in our* [Video attached] [Retweet]. Twitter. https://twitter.com/CPAC_TV/status/1631030907489353728?cxt=HHwWgICwqYD-yqItAAAA

McGregor, G. (2023, February 24). Pierre Poilievre denounces

Conservative MPs' meeting with far-right German politician. *CTVNews*. Retrieved June 17, 2023, from https://www.ctvnews.ca/politics/pierre-poilievre-denounces-conservative-mps-meeting-with-far-right-german-politician-1.6288056

McKay, J. (2023, May 4). "Business of Supply." Canada. Parliament. House of Commons. *Edited Hansard 191(1645)*. 44th Parliament, 1st session. Retrieved from the Parliament of Canada website on June 16, 2023: https://www.ourcommons.ca/DocumentViewer/en/44-1/house/sitting-191/hansard and https://openparliament.ca/debates/2023/5/4/john-mckay-1/

National Council. (2020, September 26). *Conservative Party of Canada Rules and Procedures for Candidate Nominations*. Conservative Party of Canada. Retrieved June 17, 2023, from https://cpcassets.conservative.ca/wp-content/uploads/2022/11/08152013/7afce9bba77ad0e.pdf Accessed from this webpage: https://www.conservative.ca/about-us/governing-documents/.

National Security and Intelligence Committee of Parliamentarians. (2020). National Security and Intelligence Committee of Parliamentarians Annual Report 2019 (Report No. CP100E-PDF, ISSN 2562-511X). Her Majesty the Queen in Right of Canada. Retrieved June 16, 2023, from https://www.nsicop-cpsnr.ca/reports/rp-2020-03-12-ar/intro-en.html

Newsom, S. C. (Ed.). (2002, August 5). *Burke's Speech on Conciliation with America*. Gutenburg. Retrieved June 20, 2023, from https://www.gutenberg.org/files/5655/5655-h/5655-h.htm

OTRCAT Inc. (n.d.). *The Catholic Hour*. Old Time Radio Cat (OTRCAT). Retrieved June 19, 2023, from https://www.otrcat.com/p/catholic-hour

Pardy, B. (2023, March 22). Bruce Pardy: Human rights tribunal says the quiet part out loud. *Financial Post*. Retrieved June 19, 2023, from https://financialpost.com/opinion/ontario-human-rights-tribunal-discrimination

Parliament of Canada. (n.d.). *Special Joint Committee on Medical Assistance in Dying*. Parliament of Canada — House of

Commons. Retrieved June 17, 2023, from https://www.parl.ca/Committees/en/AMAD

Pew Research Center. (2013). Canada's Changing Religious Landscape. In Pew Research Center. Retrieved June 19, 2023, from https://www.pewresearch.org/religion/2013/06/27/canadas-changing-religious-landscape/

Poilievre, P. [@PierrePoilievre]. (n.d.). *Tweets & Retweets* [Twitter profile]. Twitter. Retrieved June 17, 2023, from https://twitter.com/PierrePoilievre

Practo. (2015, March 10). *The Hippocratic Oath: The Original and Revised Version.* The Practo Blog for Doctors. Retrieved June 18, 2023, from https://doctors.practo.com/the-hippocratic-oath-the-original-and-revised-version/

Raycraft, R. (2023, April 27). Controversial bill to regulate online streaming becomes law. CBC. Retrieved June 20, 2023, from https://www.cbc.ca/news/politics/c11-online-streaming-1.6824314

Rebel News Canada. (2023, February 24). *Christine Anderson responds to criticism from Pierre Poilievre* [Video]. YouTube. Retrieved June 17, 2023, from https://www.youtube.com/watch?v=-9N4KZ9J1SQ

Schwab, K., & Malleret, T. (2020). *COVID-19: The Great Reset.* World Economic Forum.

Statistics Canada. (2021). *Insights on Canadian Society: Religiosity in Canada and its evolution from 1985 to 2019* (Catalogue number 75-006-X, ISSN 2291-0840). Retrieved from the Statistics Canada website on June 16, 2023: https://www150.statcan.gc.ca/n1/en/pub/75-006-x/2021001/article/00010-eng.pdf?st=o37719G1 and https://www150.statcan.gc.ca/n1/pub/11-627-m/11-627-m2021079-eng.htm

Steacy, L. (2023, February 22). Air Canada piloting facial recognition option for flight boarding at YVR. *CTV News Vancouver.* Retrieved June 17, 2023, from https://bc.ctvnews.ca/air-canada-piloting-facial-recognition-option-for-flight-boarding-at-yvr-1.6283695

The British Library. (2014, July 28). *English translation of Magna Carta.* The British Library. Retrieved June 19, 2023, from

175

https://www.bl.uk/magna-carta/articles/magna-carta-english-translation

The Canadian Press, & Ritchie, S. (2023, February 24). Pierre Poilievre says German politician who met with Tory MPs holds "vile" and "racist" views. National Post. Retrieved June 17, 2023, from https://nationalpost.com/news/politics/tory-leader-says-german-politician-who-met-with-mps-holds-vile-and-racist-views

The City of Calgary. (2023). *Safe & Inclusive Access Bylaw.* Calgary. Retrieved June 19, 2023, from https://www.calgary.ca/bylaws/safe-and-inclusive-access-bylaw.html

The Constitution Acts, 1867 to 1982. (1867, 30–31 Vict., c. 3 (U.K.)). British North America Act, VI. Distribution of Legislative Powers, 91–92. Retrieved from the Justice Laws of Canada website on June 19, 2023: https://laws-lois.justice.gc.ca/eng/Const/page-3.html#docCont and https://www.justice.gc.ca/eng/rp-pr/csj-sjc/constitution/lawreg-loireg/p1t13.html

The Holy Bible, New King James Version. (1982). Thomas Nelson. Retrieved July 4, 2023, from https://www.bible.com/versions/114?returnTo=JAS.2.

The Holy Bible, New International Version NIV. (2011). Biblica, Inc. Retrieved July 3, 2023, from https://www.bible.com/versions/111?returnTo=PRO.1

Tolkien, J. R. R. (1991). *The Lord of the Rings.* HarperCollins.

United Nations. (1992). United Nations Conference on Environment & Development Rio de Janerio, Brazil, 3 to 14 June 1992 — AGENDA 21. In *United Nations — Department of Economic and Social Affairs — Sustainable Development. United Nations* Sustainable Development. https://sdgs.un.org/publications/agenda21

United Nations. (2007). United Nations Declaration on the Rights of Indigenous Peoples: Resolution adopted by the General Assembly on 13 September 2007. In *United Nations* (A/RES/61/295 — (A/61/L.67 and Add.1)). Retrieved June 16, 2023, from https://social.desa.un.org/issues/indigenous-peoples/united-nations-declaration-on-the-rights-of-indigenous-peoples

United Nations. (2015). A/RES/70/1 - Transforming our world:

the 2030 Agenda for Sustainable Development. In *United Nations — Department of Economic and Social Affairs — Sustainable Development* (Seventieth session, Agenda items 15 and 116). Retrieved June 16, 2023, from https://sdgs. un.org/2030agenda and https://daccess-ods.un.org/access. nsf/Get?OpenAgent&DS=A/RES/70/1&Lang=E or https://documents-dds-ny.un.org/doc/UNDOC/GEN/ N15/291/89/PDF/N1529189.pdf?OpenElement

Wells, P. (2006). *Right Side Up: The Fall of Paul Martin and the Rise of Stephen Harper's New Conservatism.* Douglas Gibson Books.

Wells, P. (2013). *The Longer I'm Prime Minister: Stephen Harper and Canada, 2006–.* Random House Canada.

INDEX

GRANT S ABRAHAM

McKenzie, Jeremy, 118-120
Medical Assistance in Dying
(MAID), 38-40
Middle Kingdom, 25
Minor-attracted person (MAP),
36
Minorityv(including government,
party), 49-50, 57, 85, 91,
153
National security, 65, 68
National Security and
Intelligence Committee
of Parliamentarians
(NSICOP), 24, 66
NDP, 43
Nehemiah, 139-140, 146
Nihilism (moral), 35, 41-42, 64,
105, 116, 130, 142
Nuremberg Trials, 79
Official Opposition, 58, 66
Old-stock Canadian, 3, 15
O'Toole, Erin, 38, 63, 68
Parental authority, 15, 36, 38,
44-45, 62, 102, 113, 128,
146
Parliament, 31, 63, 125, 134,
150, 153, 158; building(s),
66, 92, 142; member of,
37, 134; parliamentary
committee, 40
Pied Piper, 45, 85, 133
Poilievre, Pierre, 8-9, 11, 13, 38,
40, 44-45, 52, 55-56, 58-59,
61, 63, 65, 68-69, 71, 81-
85, 94, 96, 112, 129, 133,
157-159
Politicized, 76-77, 80
Populism, 7-8, 10, 13
Populist(s) (including populist
conservatism), 7-8. 10-11,
13, 17, 57, 117
Post-nationalism, 29, 90; post
nation(al) state, 27, 51, 70;

post-nationhood, 28
Pragmatism, 49-50, 53, 115
Prima facie, 28, 83
Progressive Conservative Party, 7
Progressive Conservative Youth
Federation, 13
Prosperity, 3, 17-18, 23, 30-31,
33, 46-47, 74, 82, 115, 117,
133-134, 141, 146, 152
Prosperity index, 74, 152
Proverb, 87
Quebec Bill 15, 37
Quid pro quo, 55, 96
Rebuild(ing), 3, 33, 72, 108,
139-140
Reimer, Derek, 59-60
Reform Party, 7-9, 45, 55-56, 62
Religious freedom, 911, 15, 37,
43, 58, 62, 93-96, 113, 136;
freedom of religion, 62,
92, 109
Renaissance, 7-8, 10, 12-14, 16-
17, 111, 134
Rentier class, 16, 108, 145
Repair(ed), 16, 108, 145;
repairing, 139; unrepaired,
126
Report(s), 24, 35, 63, 66-70, 78,
83, 94, 103, 115
Reset Canada, 21
Revisionists (revisionist
historians), 26, 88, 127, 142
Riel, Louis, 108
Righteous(ness), 59-60, 143;
righteously, 59
Righteous Gentiles, 60
Rousseau, Jean-Jacques, 20
Rule by law, 77
Rule of law, 4, 21, 26, 44, 77,
87, 152
Sankey, Lord, 124-125
Schwab, Klaus, 25-26, 29
Self-determination, 127

181

This is a wake-up call to *all* Canadians.

Please consider the future of our nation and our generations if the silent majority stays silent.

-GSA

About the Author

As a voice for truth and reform, Grant Abraham has stepped forward to remind Canadians of the root values that Canada was founded upon and why these values provide an off-ramp solution to the destructive forces that are currently attempting to reshape Canada beyond recognition. He believes Canadians who align with these values are finding their voices and are finding each other in order to fuse a new expression of conservatism in Canada that radically shifts the political status quo.

Grant was born in Alberta and grew up in the Fraser Valley of British Columbia, attending high school in Abbotsford. His mother's family were homesteaders from near Kindersley, Saskatchewan; his father is a first-generation Canadian from Northern Ireland. Grant is married and has four sons.

As a qualified Barrister and Solicitor, Grant worked internationally in the area of international development and social impact investment. He is also a smallholder sheep farmer and has a keen interest in sustainable 'farm-to-fork' organic farming.

Made in the USA
Coppell, TX
11 January 2025

44252336R00108